Table of Contents

Essential Question

What can different cultures teach us?

Pinocchio

My Content Objectives

- Build vocabulary related to folktales from different cultures
- Understand what different cultures can teach

The Boy Who Cried Wolf

The Ugly Duckling

3

Word	Examples
counted (KOWN-ted)	He counted the coins. · She counted the coins.
cried (KRIDE)	The king cried, "Oh no!" · The king cried, "Help!"
gold (GOLD)	This is gold. · This is gold.
statue (STA-choo)	She is a statue. · He is a statue.

My Example	Definition
	counted, *verb* added a number of items together
	cried, *verb* yelled out sadly
	gold, *noun* a metallic material
	statue, *noun* a sculpture of a person or thing

King Midas

A Myth from Greece

The king **counted** his coins.

He made a wish.

Now everything he touched became **gold**.

The girl became a golden **statue**.

Annotate

- Circle words that you have questions about.
- Underline what happens after the king makes a wish.

"Oh no!" the king **cried**.

"Can you help?"
the king asked.

He told the king what to do.

The king was happy again.

ThinkSpeakListen
Explain what happens to the girl in this story.

King Midas

A Myth from Greece

One day, King Midas **counted** his coins and a stranger appeared.

"If I could grant you a wish, what would it be?" he asked. "I wish everything I touched turned into **gold**," King Midas replied.

The next morning, the king was thrilled when everything he touched became gold!

Then his daughter, Marigold, ran to him. But when he embraced her with a kiss, she became a golden **statue**!

"What have I done?" the king **cried**. And he wept with grief and sorrow.

"You look like the saddest man in the land," said the stranger.
"I've lost everything I care about," sobbed the king.

"Fill this pitcher with water," instructed the stranger. "Then sprinkle it on everything you've turned to gold."

King Midas followed his instructions. When everything returned to normal, the king was the happiest man ever!

ThinkSpeakListen

Reread panel 6. Explain why the stranger says that King Midas looks like "the saddest man in the land."

Remember to annotate as you read.

Notes

King Midas

A Myth from Greece

1   Long ago, there lived a king named Midas who was the richest man in the land. The king was fond of **gold** and loved it more than anything, except his daughter, Marigold.

2   One day, as King Midas **counted** his coins, a stranger appeared. "If I could grant you one wish, what would it be?" he asked.

3   "I'd wish that everything I touched turned into gold," King Midas replied.

4   "Your wish is granted!" exclaimed the stranger. "When you awake tomorrow, you'll have that power."

5   The next morning, the king awoke earlier than usual. He walked around the palace, touching every object. He was delighted and thrilled when everything he touched became gold!

6   Then Marigold ran to him. But when he embraced her with a kiss, she became a golden **statue**!

7   "What have I done?" the king **cried**. And he wept with grief and sorrow.

8   Suddenly, the stranger appeared before him. "You look like the saddest man in the land," said the stranger.

9   "I've lost everything I care about," sobbed the king.

10   "Fill this pitcher with water from the lake," instructed the stranger. "Then sprinkle it on everything you've turned into gold."

11   King Midas followed his instructions. When everything returned to normal, the king was the happiest man ever!

Identify Real-Life Connections Between Words

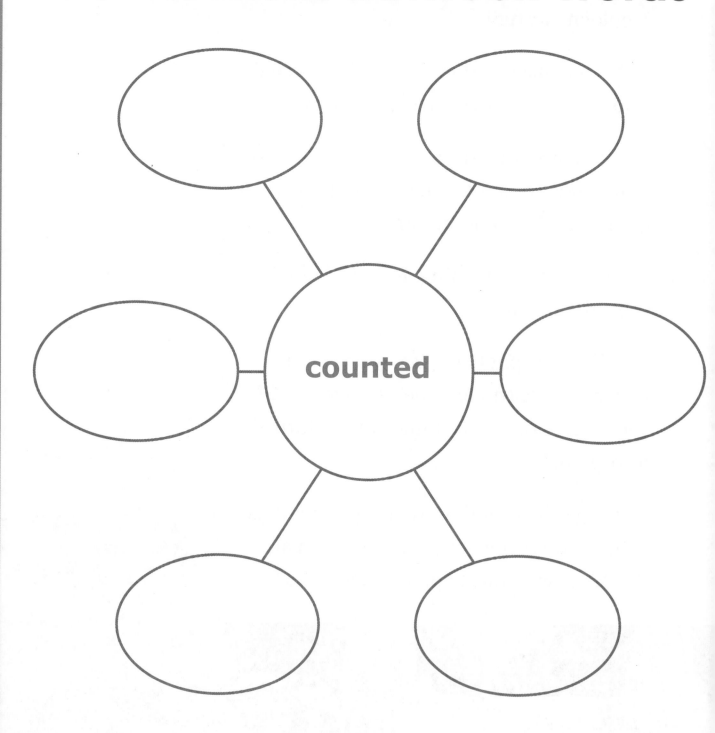

counted

Recount Story Events

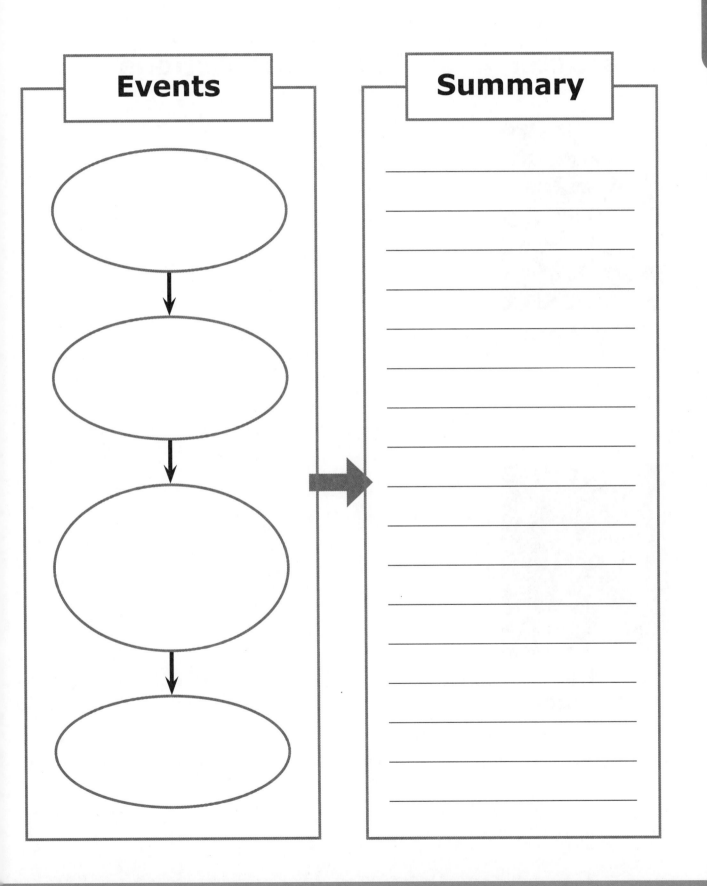

Events

Summary

Analyze Character

Character	Traits and Actions
 King Midas	
 the Stranger	

Ask and Answer Questions

1. How does the author describe Midas in the beginning of the story?

_____

Text Evidence:

_____

_____

2. When does this story take place? How do you know?

_____

Text Evidence:

_____

3. What does King Midas wish for? Why?

_____

_____

Text Evidence:

_____

_____

_____

4. How does King Midas feel when he turns his daughter into a golden statue? How does he resolve his problem?

_____

_____

Text Evidence:

_____

_____

_____

_____

Word	Examples
crops (KRAHPS)	These are crops. These are crops.
planted (PLAN-ted)	The man planted. The fox planted.
seeds (SEEDZ)	He has seeds. She has seeds.
selfish (SEL-fish)	The bear was selfish. The fox was not selfish.

My Example	Definition
	crops, *noun* plants that are grown as food
	planted, *verb* placed in the ground to grow
	seeds, *noun* things that grow into plants
	selfish, *adjective* not caring about others

A Foxy Garden

by Jeffrey Fuerst

Bear didn't want to share.

"Bear is **selfish**," said Fox.

Fox had **seeds**.

Bear and Fox **planted** the seeds.

Annotate
- Circle words that you have questions about.
- Underline how Bear is being selfish.

"We'll share the **crops**," said Fox.

"I want it all!" Bear yelled.

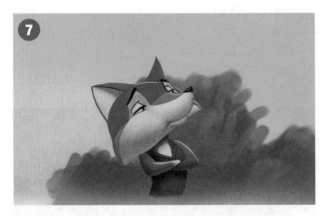

Fox said, "We will share."

Bear learned to share.

ThinkSpeakListen

Reread panel 6. How does Bear feel?

A Foxy Garden

by Jeffrey Fuerst

"Hey!" growled Bear. "Those are MY blueberries."

"Bear is being his usual **selfish** self," said Fox. "We'll have to do something about that."

Fox grabbed a handful of **seeds**. Then he went to Bear. "We'll share the **crops**," said Fox.

"How about we grow carrots?" Fox suggested.

Bear and Fox dug holes for the seeds, and the carrots grew.

Fox gave the green tops
to Bear.

"Hey!" said Bear. "I want
the orange part."

Bear roared, "I want
a new crop!"

Bear and Fox **planted** and
watered lettuce seeds.

"Now I will make a salad.
I will share it with Squirrel
and Rabbit," said Fox.

Bear felt left out.

"I was wrong not to share
the berries," said Bear. "Here
is a basket for each of you."

ThinkSpeakListen

What does Bear do at the end of the story? Why?

Notes

A Foxy Garden

by Jeffrey Fuerst

1   One day, Bear found a row of ripe blueberries by the creek. He stuffed himself and then fell asleep. Squirrel and Rabbit followed their noses to the blueberry patch, too. When they started eating the berries, Bear woke up.

2   "Hey!" growled Bear. "Those are MY blueberries."

3   Squirrel and Rabbit hightailed it back to the woods, where they told their wise friend Fox what happened.

4   "Bear is being his usual **selfish** self," said Fox. "We'll have to do something about that."

5   Fox grabbed a handful of his special, fast-growing **seeds**. Then he went to Bear and said, "I am going to plant a garden with vegetables. We'll share the **crops**. You can have everything that grows above the ground. I will get everything that grows below the ground."

6 Bear and Fox dug holes for the seeds. They **planted** and watered the carrot seeds. The carrots grew. Fox took the carrots, cut off the green tops, and gave them to Bear. "Hey!" said Bear. "I want the orange part."

7 Bear said, "I want a new crop! This time I will get the roots and the stems!"

8 Bear and Fox planted and watered lettuce seeds. The seeds grew and Bear picked armfuls of lettuce. "Not so fast," said Fox. "You are holding the leaves of lettuce."

9 "I will make a salad. I will invite Squirrel and Rabbit. We will have a picnic under the chestnut tree," said Fox.

10 Bear felt left out. He went back to the blueberry bush and picked berries. "I was wrong not to share," said Bear. "Here is a basket for each of you."

Word Web

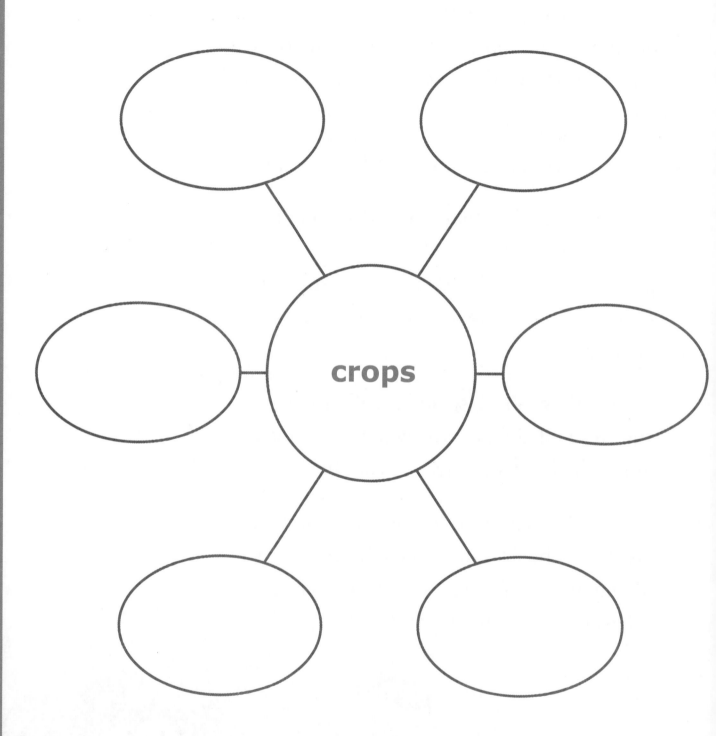

Main Message

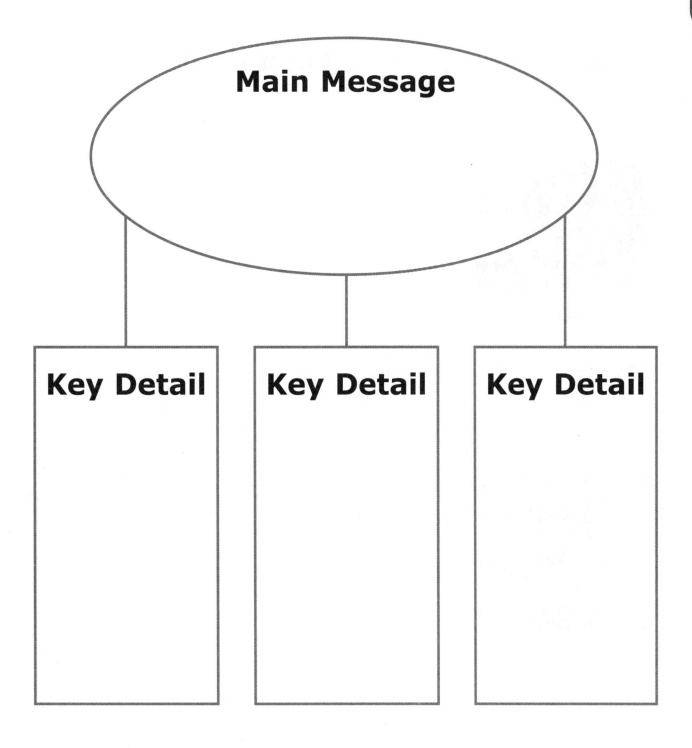

Main Message

Key Detail

Key Detail

Key Detail

Analyze Points of View

Character	Point of View
Bear	
Fox	

Recount Story Events

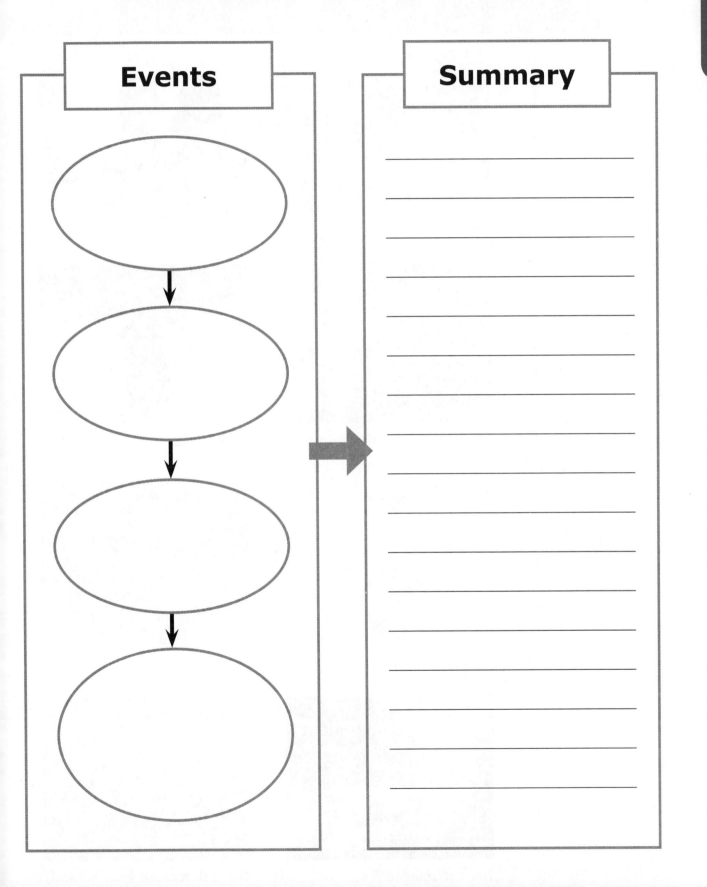

Events

Summary

Word	Examples
club (KLUB)	This is a club. This is a club.
ride (RIDE)	She can ride a unicycle. He can ride a unicycle.
unicycle (YOO-nih-sy-kul)	This is a unicycle. This is a unicycle.
zoomed (ZOOMD)	The car zoomed by. The girl zoomed by.

My Example	Definition
	club, *noun* a group of people who share a common interest
	ride, *verb* to move around
	unicycle, *noun* a cycle with only one wheel
	zoomed, *verb* sped by

On One Wheel

by Carly Schuna

1

2

"Mom," I said, "I'm not good at anything."

"You are good at riding the **unicycle**," Mom said.

3

4

"Can I bring my unicycle to school?" I asked.

"Yes, you can," Mom said.

Annotate

- Circle words that you have questions about.
- Underline clues that help you understand those words.

"What is that?" asked a girl.

"This is my unicycle.
I'm in a **club**," I said.

"Can I see you **ride** it?"
asked the girl.

I **zoomed** around
on my unicycle.

ThinkSpeakListen

Who is telling the story? How do you know?

On One Wheel

by Carly Schuna

"Mom," I said as I got into the car, "I can't do anything!"

"You're the only kid at unicycle **club** who can wheel walk," Mom said.

"Can I **ride** my **unicycle** to school today?" I asked Mom.

"Hmm," she said. "If I ride my bike next to you."

"Whoa," somebody said. "You can ride a unicycle?"

I saw Martha looking right at me. I hopped off my unicycle.

"What is that?" asked Martha. "Did you lose half your bicycle or something?"

"This is my unicycle. I ride with a club."

"Can I try?" asked Martha. Martha tried to pedal forward, but she fell off the unicycle right away.

Martha looked at me. "Can I see you do it?" she asked. I hopped on my unicycle and **zoomed** around.

ThinkSpeakListen

Explain how this story ends.

On One Wheel

by Carly Schuna

1   "Mom," I said as I got into the car, "I can't do anything!"

2   "What do you mean?" asked Mom.

3   "Martha says I can't play dodgeball."

4   "Dodgeball takes practice," said Mom. "You're good at lots of things. You can sing, you can fold origami, and you can unicycle! You're the only kid at unicycle **club** who can wheel walk," Mom added. "You're better than the grown-ups!"

5   Mom was right—I am awesome on the **unicycle**. I can do lots of fun tricks. The next morning, I woke up with an idea. "Can I **ride** my unicycle to school today?" I asked Mom.

6   "Hmm," she said. "I think that's okay, if I ride my bike next to you."

7   "Whoa!" somebody at school said. "You can ride a unicycle?"

8   Then I saw Martha looking right at me. I hopped off my unicycle.

9   "What is that?" asked Martha. "Did you lose half your bike or something?"

10   "This is my unicycle. I ride with a club. Sometimes we even perform at fairs," I said.

11   "Can I try?" asked Martha.

12   Martha tried to pedal forward, but she fell off the unicycle right away. A couple of kids snickered.

13   Martha looked at me. "Can I see you do it again?" she asked.

14   "Sure!" I said. I hopped on my unicycle and **zoomed** around forward and backward. Then I took my feet off the pedals and did my wheel walk.

Word Map

What does the word club mean?

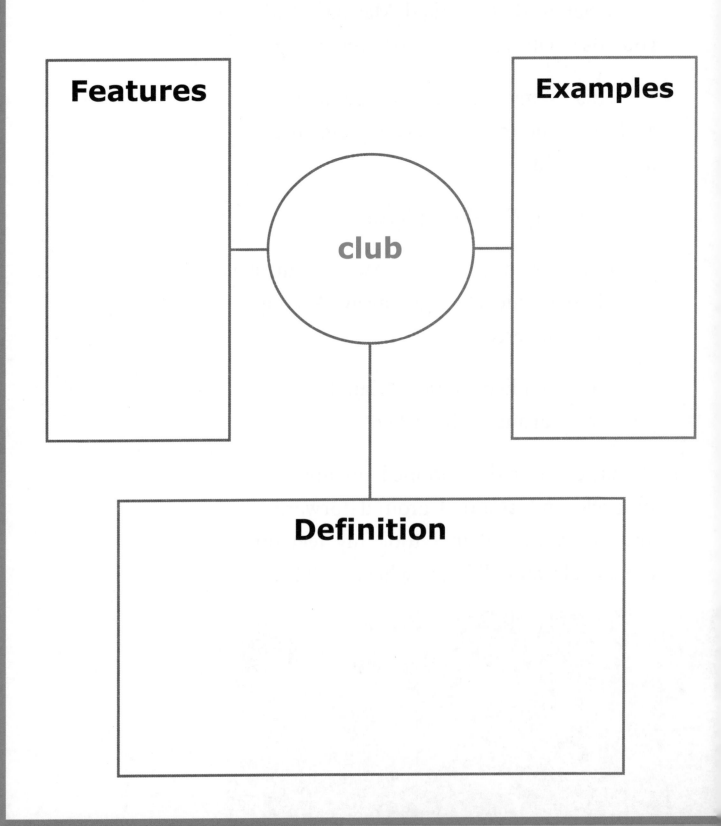

Features

Examples

club

Definition

Main Message

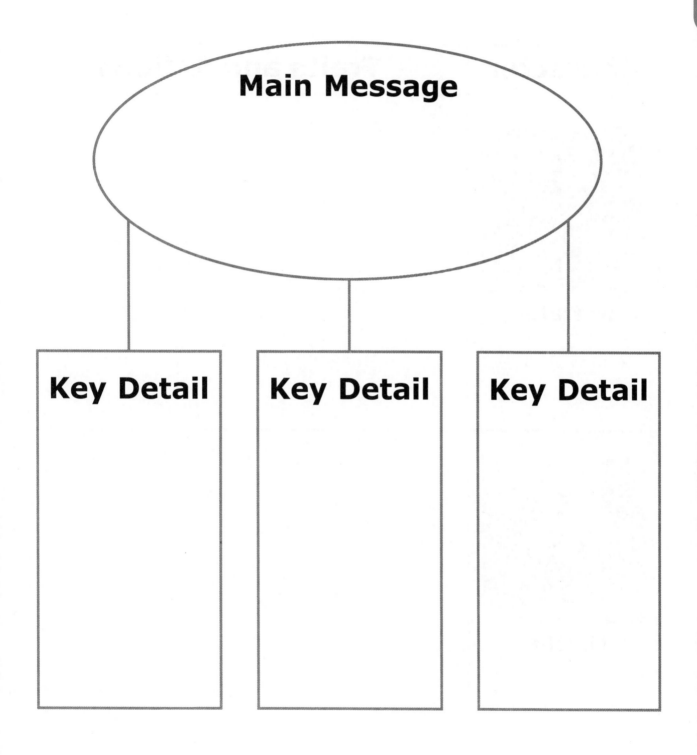

Analyze Character

Character	Traits and Actions
Narrator	
Martha	

Text Evidence Questions

1. What problem does the narrator have in the beginning of the story?

_____

Text Evidence:

_____

_____

2. What is the narrator good at? How does Mom make the narrator feel better?

_____

_____

Text Evidence:

_____

_____

_____

3. What happens when Martha tries to ride the unicycle?

_____

Text Evidence:

_____

_____

4. What lesson does this story teach you?

_____

Text Evidence:

_____

_____

Essential Question

How does understanding the past shape the future?

present and past news sources

My Content Objectives

- Build vocabulary related to learning about the past
- Understand how the past shapes our future

schoolhouse of the past

schoolhouse of the present

Word	Examples
buffalo (BUH-fuh-loh)	The buffalo runs.　　　The buffalo eats.
plain (PLANE)	The plain is large.　　　The plain is green.
trail (TRALE)	Here is a trail.　　　Here is a trail.
wagon (WA-gun)	This is a wagon.　　　This is a wagon.

My Example	Definition
	buffalo, *noun* a large wild animal
	plain, *noun* a large area of flat land
	trail, *noun* a path for people and animals to walk on
	wagon, *noun* a four-wheeled cart used for transporting people or goods

The Oregon Trail

May 17, 1849

Dear Diary,
We are on the Oregon **Trail**.

We ride in a **wagon**.

June 29, 1849

Dear Diary,
Our wagon got stuck
in the mud.

The wagon's wheel broke.

Annotate
- Circle words that you have questions about.
- Underline what happens when the wagon gets stuck in the mud.

5 July 14, 1849

Dear Diary,
We saw **buffalo** on
the **plain**.

6

We stopped at a Shoshone
(shuh-SHOH-nee) camp.

7 August 1, 1849

Dear Diary,
We are at Soda Springs!

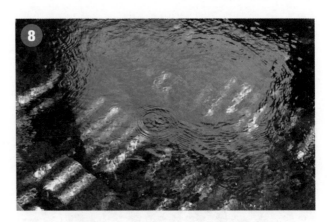

8

We will swim in the hot
springs.

—Edith

ThinkSpeakListen

Which event in the diary do you think is the most important? Why?

The Oregon Trail

May 17, 1849

Dear Diary,
We've been on the Oregon
Trail for two weeks.
I'm exhausted.

Papa and I walk while Mama
and the baby ride in the
wagon. Our weight would
be too much for the mules.

June 29, 1849

Dear Diary,
Today our wagon got stuck
in the mud. All the rain
made the trail like soup.

As a result, a wheel broke.
It was another setback.

Annotate

- Circle words that you have questions about.
- Underline how the narrator feels after traveling for two weeks.

5 July 14, 1849

Dear Diary,
At sunrise, we saw a herd of **buffalo** grazing on the **plain**.

6

Our provisions have been getting low. We stopped at a Shoshone camp and traded some iron pans for other supplies.

7 August 1, 1849

Dear Diary,
We have arrived at Soda Springs!

8

The water has bubbles in it like soda water. We are going to stay here to rest.

Yours truly, Edith

ThinkSpeakListen

Reread panel 2. Explain why the narrator and her father cannot ride in the wagon.

Remember to annotate as you read.

Notes

The Oregon Trail

May 17, 1849

Dear Diary,

We've been on the Oregon **Trail** for two weeks. I'm exhausted. Papa and I walk while Mama and the baby ride. Papa says it's because our weight would be too much for the mules.

Yours truly,
Edith

June 29, 1849

Dear Diary,

Rain, rain, and more rain! Now the trail is more like soup. Today our **wagon** got stuck in the mud. As a result, a wheel broke. It was another setback.

Yours truly,
Edith

July 14, 1849

Dear Diary,

Sunrise brought a magnificent sight—a herd of **buffalo** grazing on the **plain**. Our provisions have been getting low, so we stopped at a Shoshone camp. We traded some iron pans for other supplies.

Yours truly,
Edith

August 1, 1849

Dear Diary,

We have arrived at Soda Springs! The water has bubbles in it like soda water. We are going to stay here for an extra day because we need the rest. We can bathe in the hot springs, and Mama says the water is great for making bread.

Yours truly,
Edith

Word Map

What does the word trail mean?

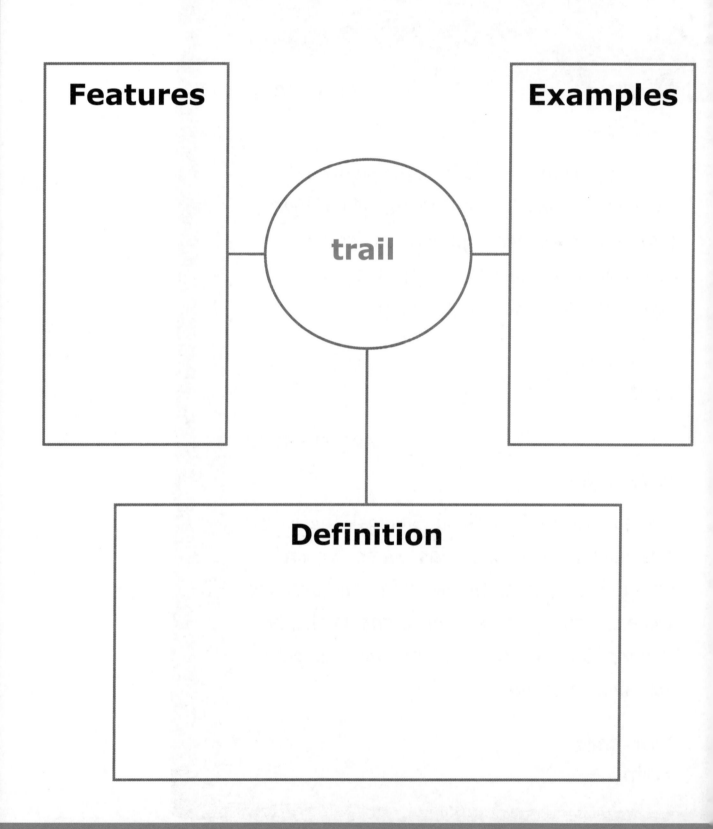

Features

Examples

trail

Definition

Main Idea

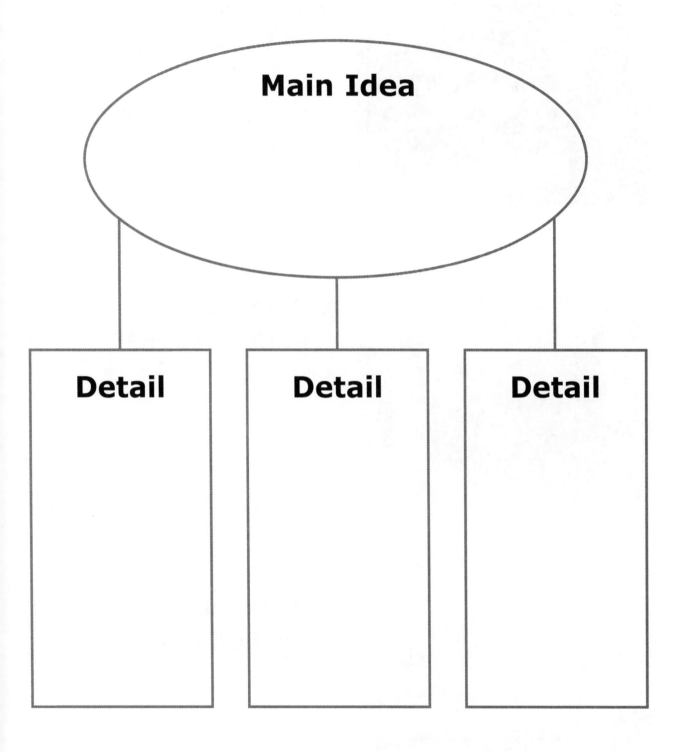

Use Graphic Features

1 **What do you see in the picture?**

_____

_____

_____

2 **Who rides in the wagon?**

_____

_____

_____

3 **Where are the buffalo?**

_____

_____

_____

Cause and Effect

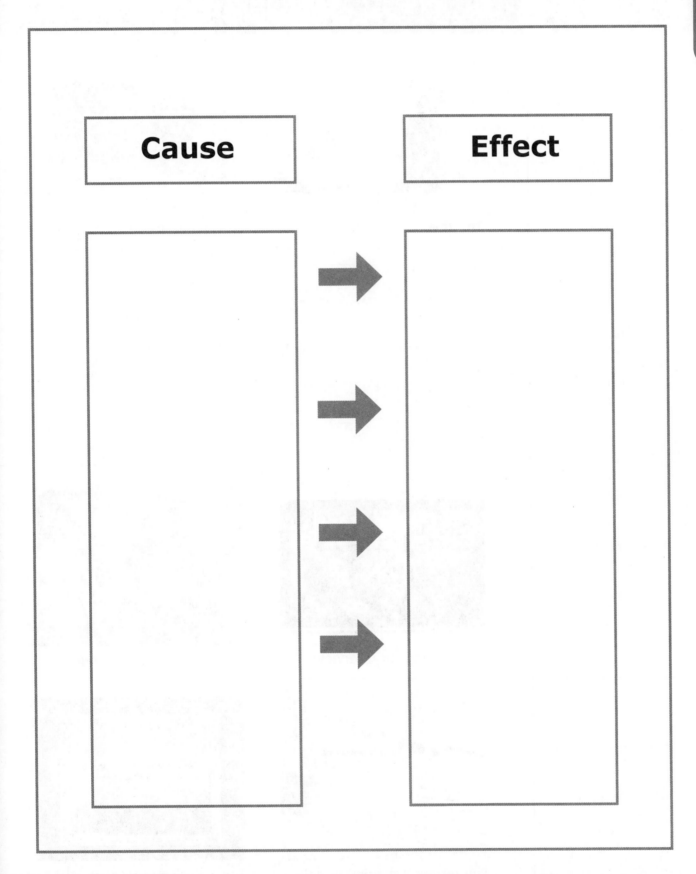

Cause		Effect

Word	Examples
artifacts (AR-tih-fakts)	The toys are artifacts. The tools are artifacts.
diary (DY-uh-ree)	This is a diary. This is a diary.
interview (IN-ter-vyoo)	He is giving an interview. She is giving an interview.
primary sources (PRY-mair-ee SOR-sez)	The letters are primary sources. The paintings are primary sources.

54

My Example	Definition
	artifacts, *noun* objects from the past
	diary, *noun* a book in which people write their experiences
	interview, *noun* a meeting between two or more people where questions are asked
	primary sources, *noun* firsthand accounts

Primary Sources

by Margaret McNamara

1

We use **primary sources** to learn about the past.

2

A primary source gives us information.

3

An **interview** is a primary source. We can listen to or watch interviews.

4

A painting is a primary source. It can show a past event.

Annotate

- Circle words that you have questions about.
- Underline clues that help you understand what those words mean.

We can look at photographs. They are primary sources, too.

Many people keep **diaries**. A diary is a primary source.

Artifacts are primary sources. These tools are from the past.

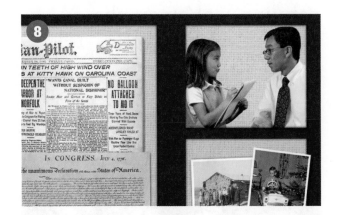

We can learn a lot from primary sources.

ThinkSpeakListen

Explain what types of artifacts you see in panel 7.

Primary Sources

by Margaret McNamara

We learn about the past by using **primary sources**. You can look at **interviews**, paintings, photographs, writings, and **artifacts**.

A primary source is someone who has direct knowledge of a topic.

A reporter's interview is a primary source. You can listen to interviews or read interviews in newspapers or magazines.

Before photography, people painted and drew pictures. Paintings are primary sources of information.

5

Photography is an important way to record events. Photographs are primary sources for topics from the past.

6

Diaries, newspapers, and letters are primary sources. They are good ways to learn about the past.

7

Artifacts are primary sources too. We can learn about how people lived and worked by looking at old tools.

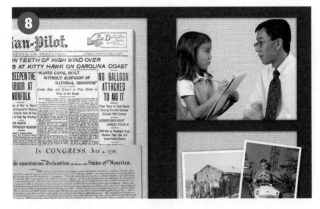

8

How do you find out about the past? One of the best ways is to find primary sources.

ThinkSpeakListen

In panel 5, what type of primary source helps you learn about the past?

Notes

Primary Sources

by Margaret McNamara

1 How do you find out about something from the past? One of the best ways is to find **primary sources**. *Primary* means "firsthand." A primary source is someone who has direct knowledge of the topic. Someone who lived through an event is a primary source. You can **interview** that person about the event. You can also look for paintings, photographs, writings, and **artifacts**.

2 An interview is when you ask someone questions. A reporter's interview is a primary source. You can watch interviews on TV. You can listen to some interviews on the radio or the Internet. You can read other interviews in newspapers or in magazines.

artifacts | photograph | letter

3   Photography did not exist until the 1800s. Before then people painted and drew pictures of other people. They painted important events. These paintings are primary sources of information. They show how people lived long ago.

4   Photographs are good primary sources for topics from the past. They are good primary sources for things that happen today, too.

5   The written word is another primary source. In the past, people sent handwritten letters to one another. Now they send e-mails. **Diaries**, newspapers, and documents are other forms of the written word.

6   Artifacts are things made by people. They are another important primary source. We can learn about how people lived and worked by looking at old tools. Artifacts show what daily life was like in the past. Old toys tell us how people used to have fun!

Word Map

What does primary sources mean?

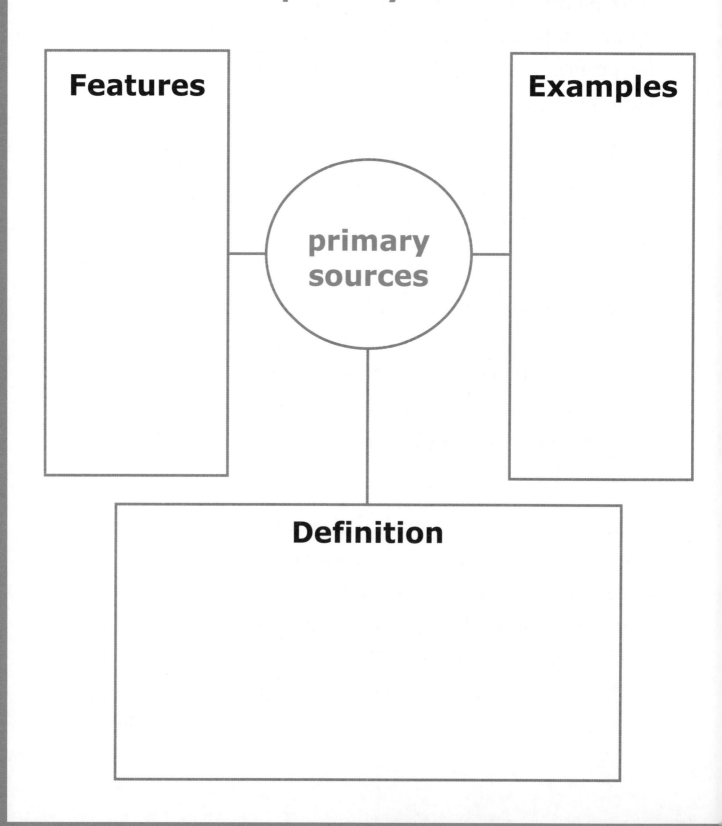

Features

Examples

primary sources

Definition

Main Idea

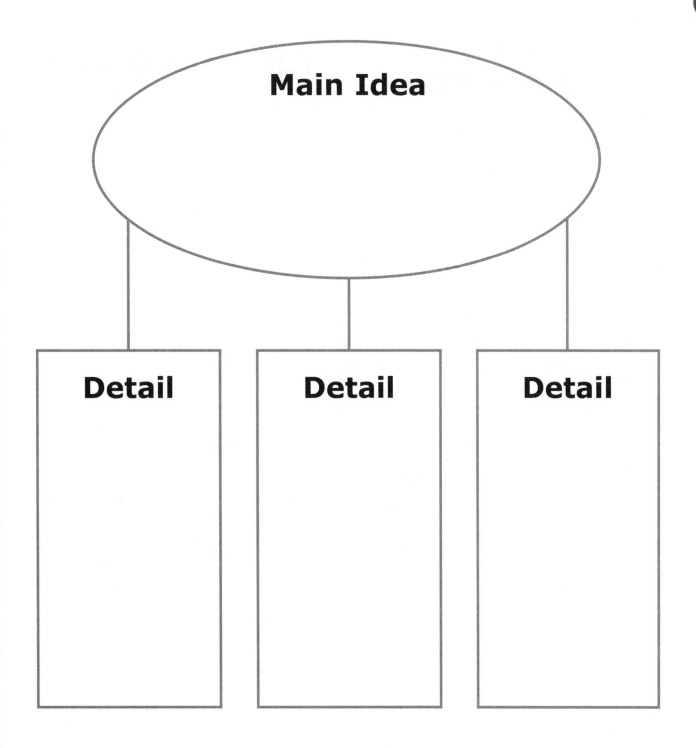

Analyze Author's Purpose

Author's Statement	Facts and Details

Compare and Contrast

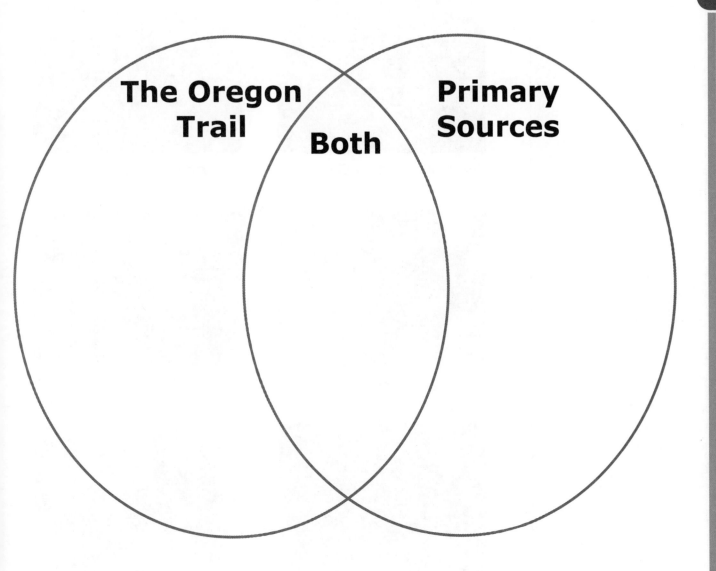

The Oregon Trail

Both

Primary Sources

Word	Examples	
cliff (KLIF)	The rocks are on a cliff.	The people are on a cliff.
dig (DIG)	She is at the dig.	He is at the dig.
fossil (FAH-sul)	This is a fossil.	This is a fossil.
skull (SKUL)	This is a skull.	This is a skull.

My Example	Definition
	cliff, *noun* a steep ledge
	dig, *noun* a place where people look for animal remains
	fossil, *noun* the remains of an animal or plant from many years ago
	skull, *noun* the bones of the head

My Summer Dig

by Terri Patterson

August 11, 1990

We are at the **dig**.

August 12, 1990

We found bones on a **cliff**.

We named the dinosaur SUE after the woman who found it.

August 14, 1990

We used tools to get to the bones.

Annotate
- Circle words that you have questions about.
- Underline what they found on the cliff.

August 18, 1990

Today we got down to the **fossil**.

We used tools to remove the bones.

August 23, 1990

We dug out the **skull** today.

September 1, 1990

We left the dig today. It took seventeen days to dig SUE out.

ThinkSpeakListen

Reread panel 8. Explain how long it took to dig SUE out.

My Summer Dig

by Terri Patterson

August 11, 1990

Tomorrow is the last day of the **dig**. We dug up many dinosaur bones.

August 12, 1990

Sue found some huge bones sticking out of a **cliff**. They were too big to be anything but a *T. rex*!

The ground was covered with pieces of bone. We named the dinosaur SUE after the person who found it.

August 14, 1990

Early this morning, we got started digging up the *T. rex*. We used picks to break up smaller rocks and shovels to move dirt.

August 18, 1990

Our hard work over the past few days finally paid off. Today we got down to the **fossil**.

We used small hand tools to remove the dirt and rock around the bones.

August 23, 1990

Pete dug out the **skull** today. It's almost five feet long! He thinks that this *T. rex* was a giant.

September 1, 1990

We left the dig today. It took seventeen days to dig SUE out. All the bones are finally on their way to the lab.

ThinkSpeakListen

Explain why different parts of the dig need different tools.

Notes

My Summer Dig

by Terri Patterson

1   **August 11, 1990**

Tomorrow is the last day of the **dig**. I can't believe I've been in South Dakota for ten weeks. We dug up many dinosaur bones. Some are more than sixty million years old!

2   **August 12, 1990**

What a day! Sue found some huge bones sticking out of a **cliff**. They were too big to be anything but a dinosaur. In this part of the world, it could only be a T. rex! The ground below the cliff was covered with pieces of bone. More than ten bones stuck out of the cliff. Pete thought that a whole skeleton might be buried there.

The bones are under almost thirty feet of dirt and rock. It's going to take a lot of hard work to remove the skeleton.

3 **August 14, 1990**

Early this morning, we got started digging up the T. rex, which we named SUE. A machine might break or crush a **fossil**, so we did all the work by hand. We used picks to break up smaller rocks and shovels to move dirt.

4 **August 18, 1990**

Today we got down to the fossils. We used small hand tools to remove the dirt and rock around the bones.

5 **August 23, 1990**

Pete dug out the **skull** today. It's almost five feet long! He thinks that this T. rex was a giant. Its bones are bigger than any T. rex he has seen.

6 **September 1, 1990**

We left the dig today. It took seventeen days to dig SUE out of the ground.

All the bones are finally on their way to the lab. It will take a long time to clean up the skeleton.

Word Web

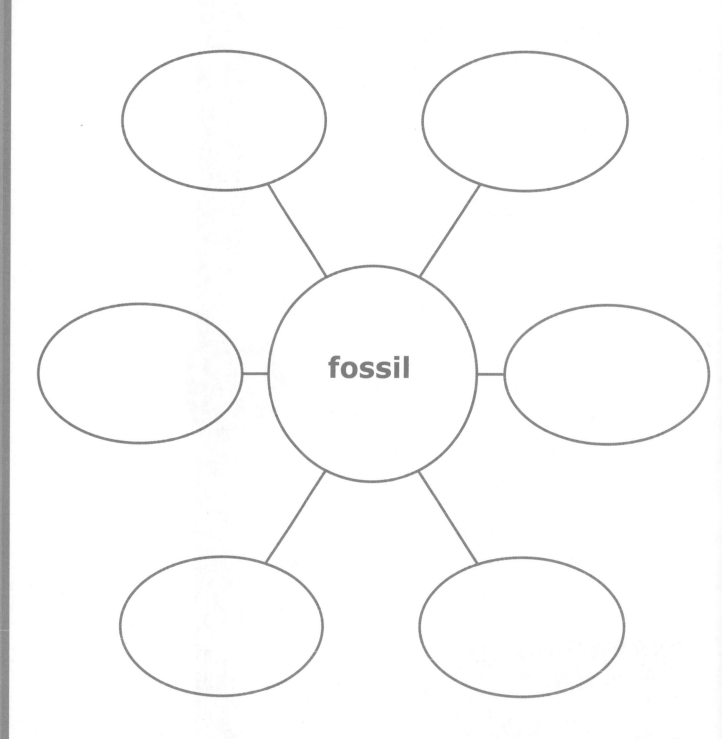

fossil

Main Idea

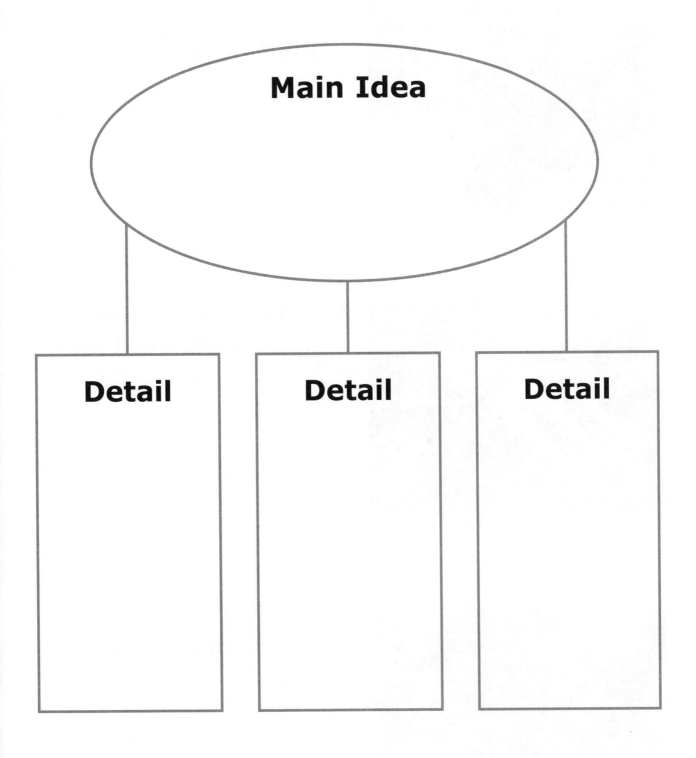

Use Graphic Features

1 Who is in this photograph?

_____

_____

_____

2 What were small hand tools used for?

_____

_____

_____

3 What do you see in this photograph?

_____

_____

_____

Ask and Answer Questions

1. How long was the author in South Dakota? What was she doing there?

_____

Text Evidence:

_____

_____

2. What happened on August 12, 1990?

_____

Text Evidence:

_____

_____

_____

3. What did they use to dig up the _T. rex_?

_____

Text Evidence:

_____

_____

_____

4. How long did it take them to dig out SUE?

_____

_____

Text Evidence:

_____

_____

Essential Question

How do we react to changes in nature?

natural bridge

My Content Objectives

- Build vocabulary related to changes in nature
- Understand the processes that change nature

mountains
in Alaska

rocky cliffs

79

Word	Examples	
canyon (KAN-yun)	 The canyon is large.	 The canyon is deep.
erosion (ih-ROH-zhun)	 The water caused erosion.	 The wind caused erosion.
mudslide (MUD-slide)	 This is a mudslide.	 This is a mudslide.
visit (VIH-zit)	 They visit the canyon.	 They visit the canyon.

My Example	Definition
	canyon, *noun* a deep gorge
	erosion, *noun* the wearing away of Earth's surface by water or wind
	mudslide, *noun* mud and dirt flowing on land
	visit, *verb* to go to a place

Water's Awesome Wonder

When water wears away rock, it is called "**erosion**."

The Grand **Canyon** was formed by erosion.

The **mudslides** cut away more rock.

The canyon is more than a mile deep.

Annotate
- Circle words that you have questions about.
- Underline how the Grand Canyon was formed.

5

Some people **visit** the Grand Canyon.

6

They go on mule rides.

7

The Grand Canyon is more than a hole in the ground.

8

It is a sculpture made by nature.

ThinkSpeakListen

Tell key details from "Water's Awesome Wonder."

Water's Awesome Wonder

When water moves over rock, it slowly wears away the rock. We call that "**erosion**."

The Grand **Canyon** began to form long ago. The Colorado River flowed across the desert floor, carving through the rock in its path.

Wind, sand, and **mudslides** cut away even more rock. Slowly the gash became deeper and deeper.

Today this beautiful canyon is more than a mile deep in some places.

People **visit** the Grand Canyon because it is one of the most beautiful places on Earth. It has unusually shaped rocks and colorful canyon walls.

Mule rides, hiking, and rafting down the Colorado River are three exciting ways for visitors to see the fantastic shapes and colors of the canyon.

Erosion and weathering created something beautiful in Arizona's desert. The Grand Canyon is more than just a deep hole in the ground.

It is a sculpture that has been carved over five million years by the mighty forces of nature.

ThinkSpeakListen

Reread panel 2. Explain how the Colorado River helped form the Grand Canyon.

Notes

Water's Awesome Wonder

1   Did you know that water can be an artist? It can when it flows downhill and carves rock into amazing shapes!

2   When water moves over rock, it slowly wears away the rock. We call that "**erosion**." In my opinion, erosion can create something beautiful. The Grand **Canyon** is a great example of this!

3   The Grand Canyon began to form long ago. The Colorado River flowed across the desert floor, carving through the rock in its path. Wind, sand, and **mudslides** cut away even more rock. Slowly the gash became deeper and deeper.

4   Today this beautiful canyon is more than a mile deep in some places. It can even be seen from space.

5   People **visit** the Grand Canyon for many reasons. It is one of the most beautiful places on Earth, with its unusually shaped rocks and colorful canyon walls.

6   Mule rides, hiking, and rafting down the Colorado River are three exciting ways for visitors to see the fantastic shapes and colors of the canyon.

7   The Grand Canyon is so much more than just a deep hole in the ground. It is a sculpture that has been carved over five million years by the mighty forces of nature. And it is still being shaped today!

The Colorado River has been carving the Grand Canyon for over five million years.

Word Web

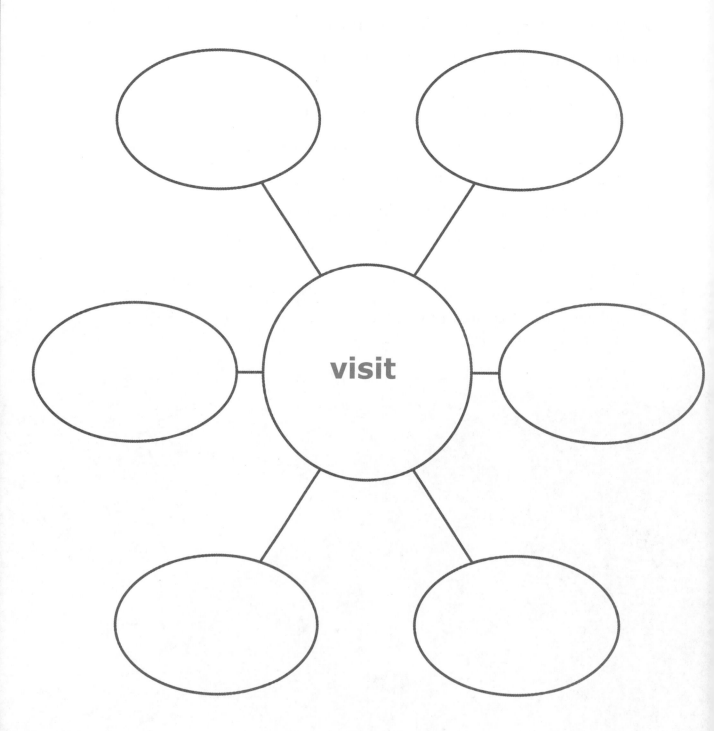

Main Idea

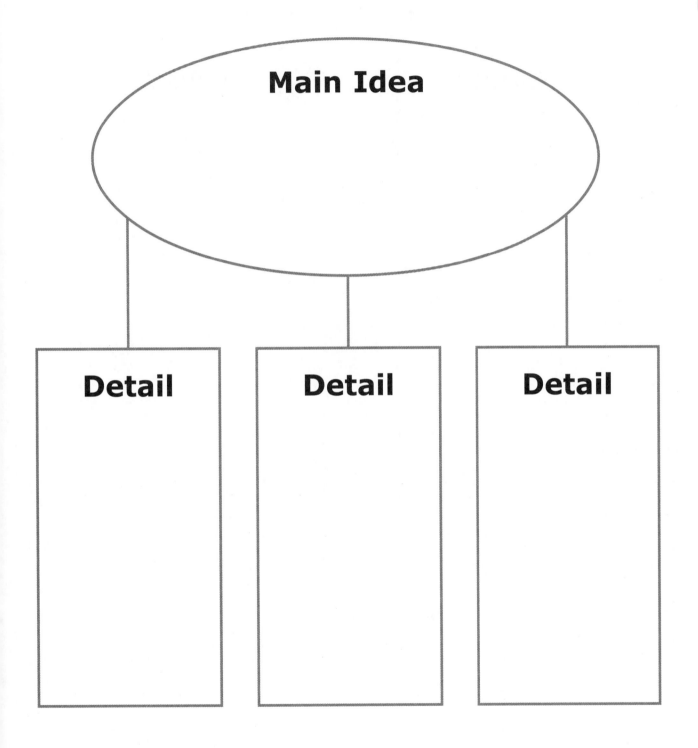

Cause and Effect

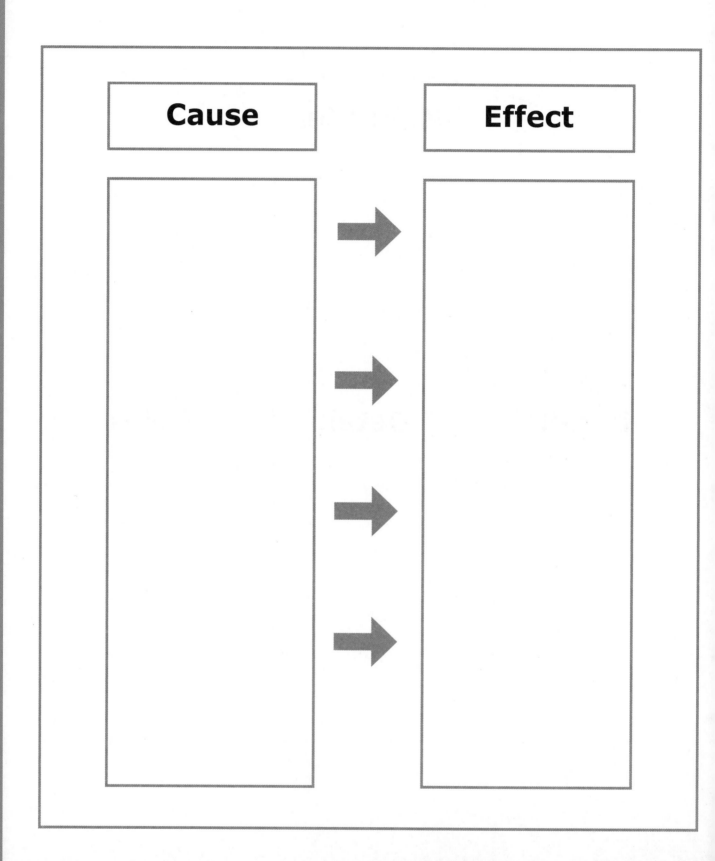

Cause		Effect

Analyze Reasons and Evidence

In my opinion, erosion can create something beautiful.

Reasons	Evidence

Word	Examples
crops (KRAHPS)	These are crops. These are crops.
damage (DA-mij)	The tree has damage. The house has damage.
flood (FLUD)	This is a flood. This is a flood.
storm (STORM)	The storm has strong wind. The storm has heavy rain.

My Example	Definition
	crops, *noun* plants that are grown as food
	damage, *noun* harm done to property
	flood, *noun* an overflowing of water
	storm, *noun* bad weather

Earth's Changes

by Louise Carroll

The strong wind and flowing water cause erosion.

The wearing away of Earth's surface is erosion.

The waves cause erosion to the rocks.

A **storm** can cause a **flood**.

Annotate

- Circle words that you have questions about.
- Underline what causes erosion.

These walls are built
to prevent flooding.

The strong wind can
hurt **crops**.

A wall of trees helps prevent
wind erosion.

A lot of **damage** is
caused by erosion.

ThinkSpeakListen

Explain some ways that erosion can change Earth's surface.

Earth's Changes

by Louise Carroll

When water wears away sand, soil, or rock, it is called "erosion." Strong winds can also cause erosion.

Erosion wears away Earth's surface. It changes the way Earth looks.

Earth has oceans, rivers, lakes, and streams. Ocean waves crashing against rocks cause erosion.

Storms can bring so much rain that rivers and lakes overflow. Then water runs over the land, causing a **flood**.

Walls can be built around rivers that flood when it rains heavily. A wall can also keep ocean waves from striking land.

Wind erosion is not good for farmers' **crops**. Wind blows away the top layer of soil.

A wall of trees can help slow wind erosion. The trees can block the wind from blowing away the crops.

Water and wind can cause a lot of **damage** to Earth. They can cause damage to people's things, too.

ThinkSpeakListen

Reread panel 6. Describe what wind erosion can do to crops.

Earth's Changes

by Louise Carroll

1   Over time, flowing water wears away the surrounding rock and soil. When water wears away sand, soil, or rock, it is called "erosion." Strong winds can also cause erosion. Erosion wears away Earth's surface. It changes the way Earth looks.

2   Earth has oceans, rivers, lakes, and streams. Ocean water slowly wears away the shoreline. Ocean waves crashing against rocks can also cause erosion.

3   Sometimes water can change the land in a short amount of time. **Storms** can bring so much rain that rivers and lakes overflow. Then water runs over the land. This is called a "**flood**." Floodwater pushes things in its way. The land changes from the force of the moving water.

4　　Walls can be built around rivers that flood when it rains heavily. A wall can also keep ocean waves from striking land. Sometimes homes are built close to shore. A wall can keep them safe from ocean water.

5　　Wind erosion is not good for farmers' **crops**. Wind blows away the top layer of soil. That layer has things in it that help plants grow. A wall of trees can help slow wind erosion. It can help keep farmers' crops healthy. The trees can block the wind from blowing away the crops.

6　　Water and wind can cause a lot of **damage** to Earth. They can cause damage to people's things too.

Word Map

What does the word storm mean?

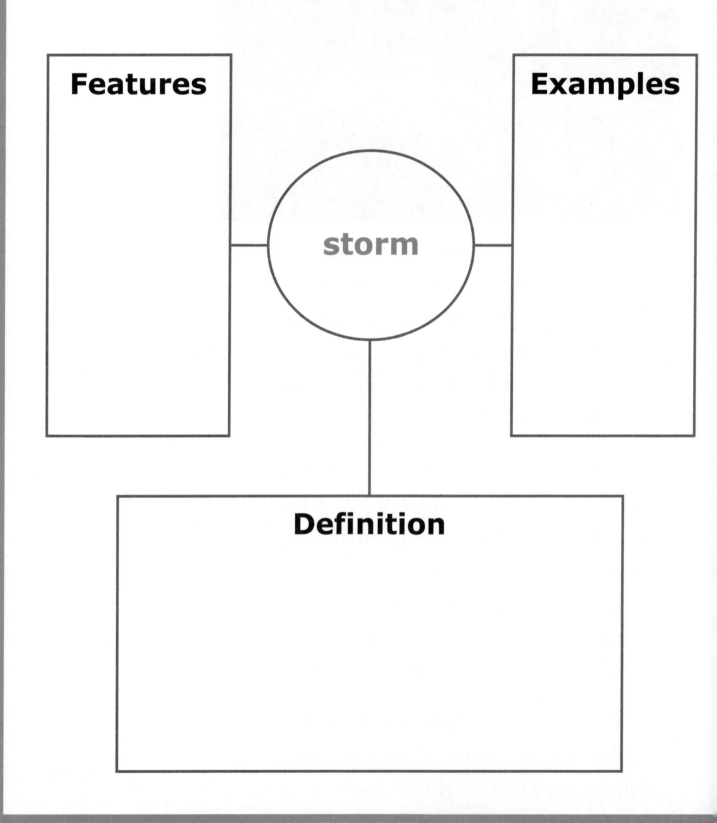

Features

Examples

storm

Definition

Main Idea

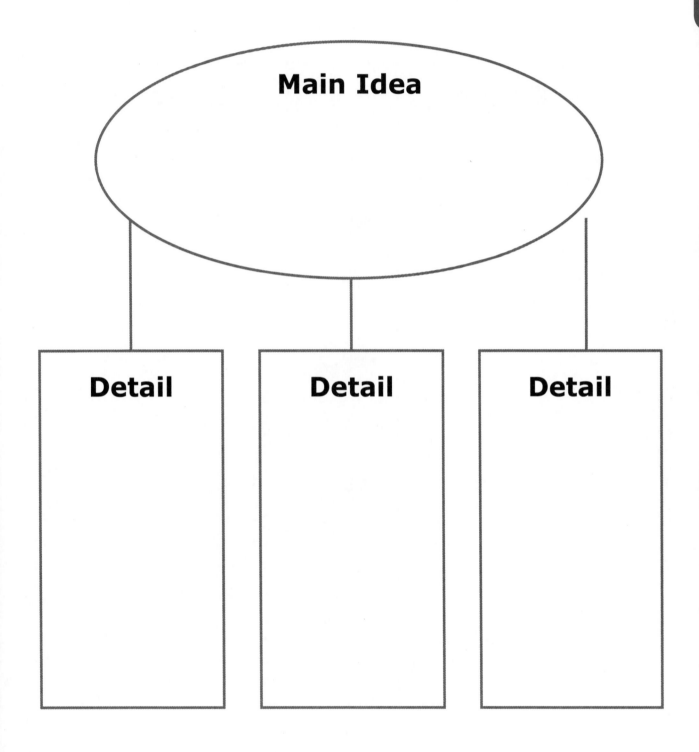

Cause and Effect

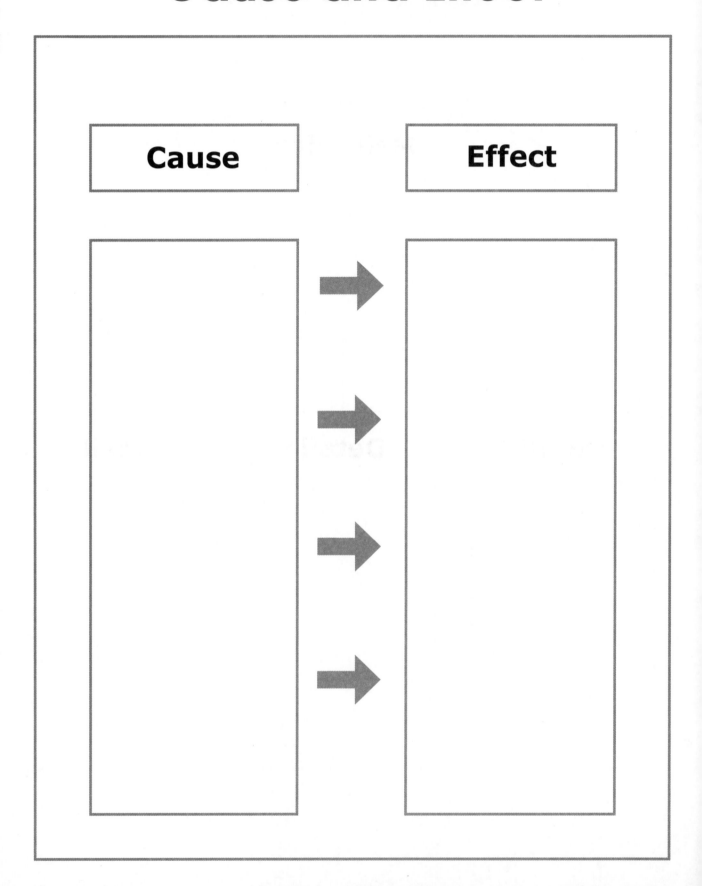

Cause

Effect

Compare and Contrast

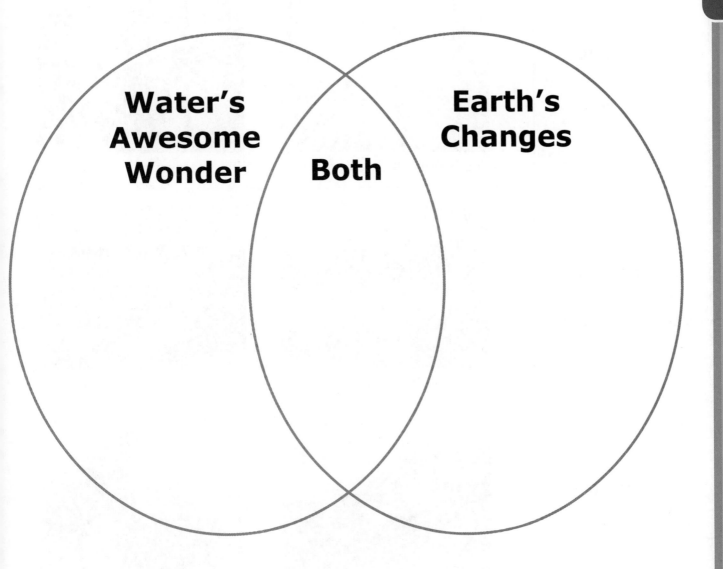

Water's
Awesome
Wonder

Both

Earth's
Changes

Word	Examples
boardwalk (BORD-wauk)	 The boardwalk is empty.  The boardwalk is crowded.
nature preserve (NAY-cher prih-ZERV)	 This is a nature preserve.  This is a nature preserve.
rebuild (ree-BILD)	 They had to rebuild.  They had to rebuild.
report (rih-PORT)	 She gives a report.  He gives a report.

My Example	Definition
	boardwalk, *noun* a wooden walkway near the beach
	nature preserve, *noun* a protected area of land for plants and animals
	rebuild, *verb* to build again
	report, *noun* a spoken or written account

Surf Haven Debates Its Future

by Jay Forte

The **boardwalk** was damaged by a storm.

The man gave a **report**.

The town wanted to **rebuild** the boardwalk.

"We should not rebuild. We should make a **nature preserve**."

Annotate
- Circle words that you have questions about.
- Underline what caused the damage to the boardwalk.

"We should not rebuild.
We will have more storms."

"We should not rebuild.
We should have a place
for wildlife."

"If we rebuild, we will
have jobs."

"We can have a nature
preserve and shops."

ThinkSpeakListen

In panel 8, how does the woman solve the problem?

Surf Haven Debates Its Future

by Jay Forte

When Hurricane Stanley hit, the small town of Surf Haven took a pounding. Stanley's powerful winds ripped up the historic **boardwalk**.

Town councilman Matt Fenton gave a **report**. "Forty businesses were destroyed," he said. "We need fifty million dollars to repair the damage."

Mayor Jan Brill said the town should **rebuild** the boardwalk. "Visitors come here every summer. They spend millions of dollars."

Dr. Kay Smith disagreed. "Ocean levels are rising. We should turn the boardwalk into a **nature preserve**."

5 Local weather expert Tom Lee agreed. "In ten years, the water could rise two more inches. That means we will have even worse flooding during storms."

6 John Garcia gave other reasons for making a nature preserve. "What people need is a beautiful sandy beach and wildlife."

7 Shop owner Phil Pippin objected. "I have ten employees who need a paycheck. What will they do?"

8 Jackie Obler tried to calm the audience. "We could have a nature preserve and shops nearby. I can help."

ThinkSpeakListen

Describe the kinds of damage a hurricane can cause.

Surf Haven Debates Its Future

by Jay Forte

1   When Hurricane Stanley hit land last week, the small town of Surf Haven took a pounding. Stanley's powerful winds ripped up the historic **boardwalk**. High waves flooded the seashore shops.

2   Last night, Surf Haven's mayor, Jan Brill, held a meeting about the boardwalk's future. Town councilman Matt Fenton gave a damage **report**. "Forty businesses were destroyed," he said. "Twenty others were badly flooded. The town has lost three hundred jobs. We need fifty million dollars to repair the damage."

3   Mayor Jan Brill said the town should **rebuild** the boardwalk. "Our future is at stake. Visitors come here every summer. They spend millions of dollars. If we don't rebuild, they won't come. Our town depends on the visitors. They come to see our historic boardwalk."

4   Dr. Kay Smith from the Climate Study Group disagreed. "Ocean levels are rising. Weather patterns are changing. Rebuilding the boardwalk is a waste of money. We should turn the boardwalk into a **nature preserve**."

5   Local weather expert Tom Lee agreed. "The National Weather Panel says that in ten years, the water could rise two more inches. That means we will have even worse flooding during storms."

6   Resident John Garcia gave other reasons for making a nature preserve. "What people need is a beautiful sandy beach and wildlife. We should build a nature preserve."

7   Shop owner Phil Pippin objected. "My shop has been there for fifty years. I have ten employees who need a paycheck. What will they do? What will their families do?"

8   Business owner Jackie Obler tried to calm the audience. "We could build new shops away from the shoreline. We could have a nature preserve and shops nearby. I can help."

Use Prefixes to Determine Word Meaning

Word	Prefix	Prefix Meaning	Word Meaning

Main Idea

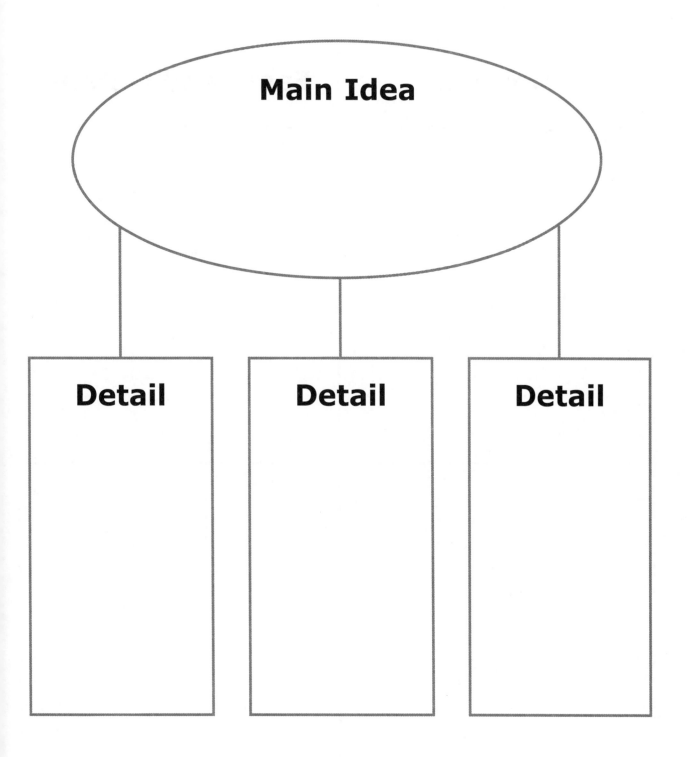

Analyze Opinion

Opinion	Facts and Details

Analyze Reasons and Evidence

Should Surf Haven rebuild the boardwalk?

Reason	Evidence

Essential Question

How do the goods we make, buy, and sell connect us?

cornfield

My Content Objectives

- Build vocabulary related to producing, buying, and selling goods
- Understand how the exchange of goods shapes communities

man picking corn

woman selling corn

117

Word	Examples
business (BIZ-nes)	The bear is in business. The goat is in business.
customers (KUS-tuh-merz)	The customers buy food. The customers buy food.
earn (ERN)	They earn money. They earn money.
purchased (PER-chest)	The goat purchased a potato. The bear purchased a bun.

My Example	Definition
	business, *noun* a job that provides goods or services
	customers, *noun* people who buy goods
	earn, *verb* to get in return for work
	purchased, *verb* bought

Goat and Bear in Business

Goat and Bear went into **business** to **earn** money.

"I'm going to sell potatoes," said Bear.

"I'll sell buns," said Goat.

They waited for **customers**. Soon Goat was hungry. He **purchased** one of Bear's potatoes.

Annotate

- Circle words that you have questions about.
- Underline clues that help you understand those words.

Bear was hungry, too. He bought one of Goat's buns. Now Goat had money. He purchased another potato from Bear.

Goat and Bear counted their money. They had only one nickel!

ThinkSpeakListen

Tell what happens first, next, and last in the story.

Goat and Bear in Business

Goat and Bear decided to go into **business** so they could **earn** some money. "I'm going to sell my delicious baked potatoes!" said Bear.

"I'll sell my delectable raisin buns!" exclaimed Goat.

They waited for the **customers** to arrive. Before long, Goat was hungry. He had a nickel in his pocket, so he **purchased** one of Bear's potatoes.

Annotate
- Circle words that you have questions about.
- Underline clues that help you understand those words.

Soon Bear was hungry, too. So he took the nickel he had earned and bought one of Goat's raisin buns. Goat was delighted with his first sale! Now he had a nickel. To celebrate, he purchased another potato from Bear.

Goat and Bear went back and forth in the same way. However, when they counted their money, they didn't understand how they could have only one nickel!

Notes

Goat and Bear in Business

1   Goat and Bear were best friends. One day, the two decided to go into **business** so they could **earn** some money.

2   "I'm going to sell my delicious baked potatoes!" said Bear.

3   "I'll sell my delectable raisin buns!" exclaimed Goat.

4   "I'm sure we'll do very well," declared Bear.

5   "We'll be very successful!" added Goat.

6   The next morning, they went to the market to sell their goods. After they set out their food, they waited for the **customers** to arrive. Before long, Goat was hungry. He had a nickel in his pocket, so he **purchased** one of Bear's potatoes.

7   Soon Bear was hungry, too. So he took the nickel he had earned and bought one of Goat's raisin buns.

8   Goat was delighted with his first sale! Now he had a nickel. To celebrate, he purchased another potato from Bear. By the time Goat had finished the potato, Bear was back to buy another raisin bun for a nickel.

9   All afternoon, Goat and Bear went back and forth in the same way. By the end of the day, they were pleased to see that all their food was gone. However, when they counted their money, the two friends were puzzled. They didn't understand how they could sell everything and have only one nickel!

Word Map

What does the word business mean?

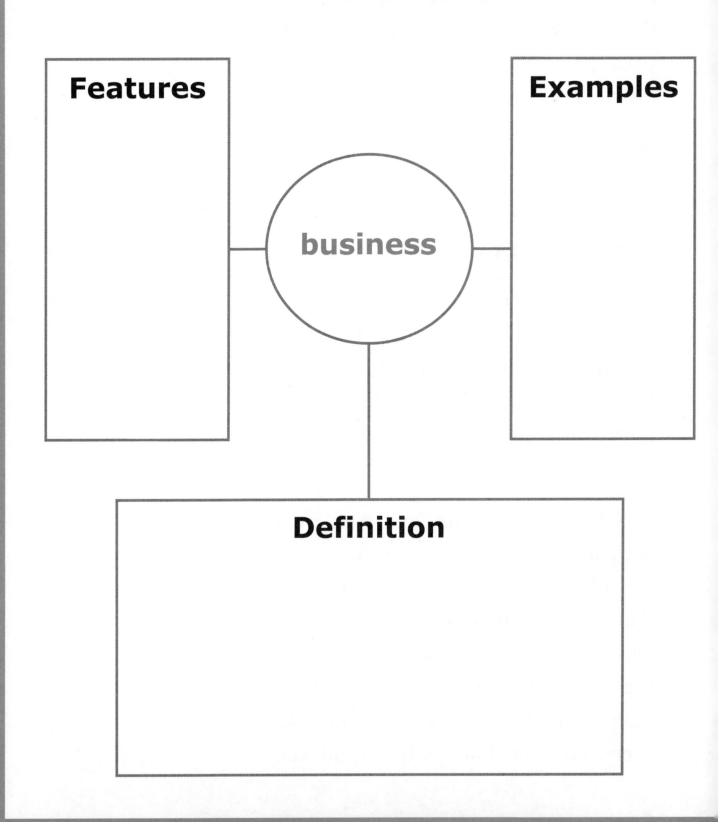

Features

Examples

business

Definition

Determine Central Message

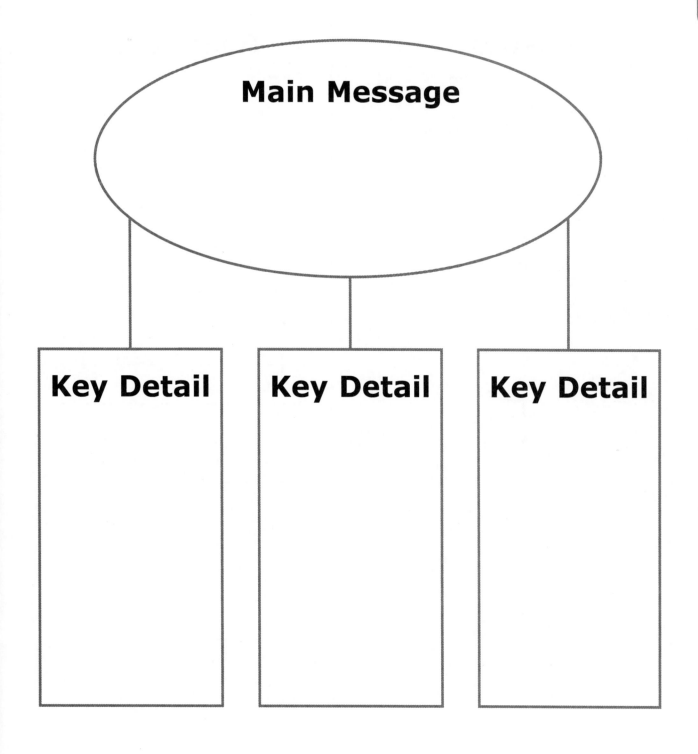

Main Message

Key Detail

Key Detail

Key Detail

Recount Story Events

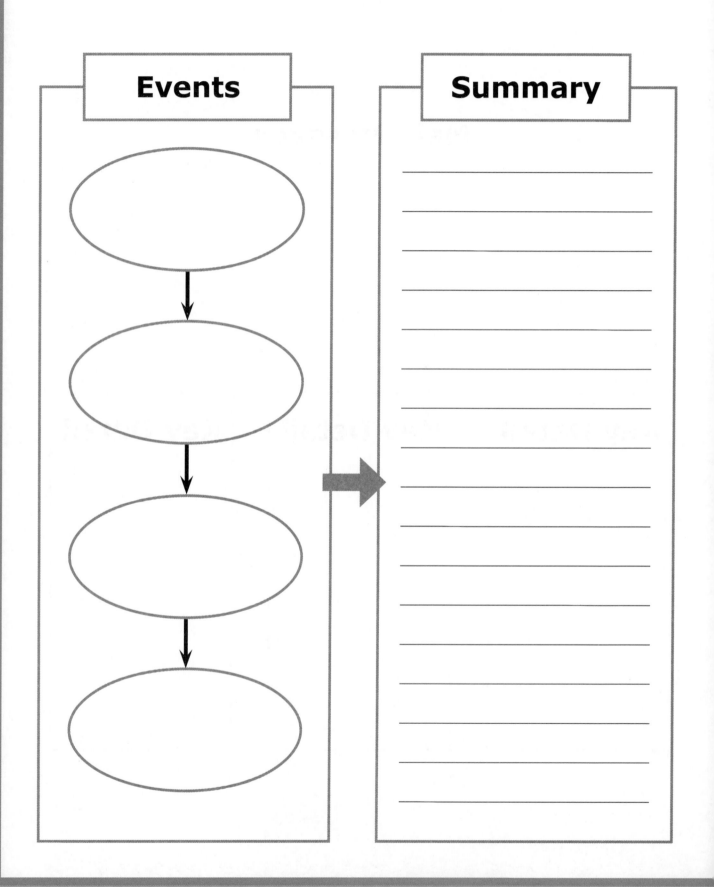

Events

Summary

Ask and Answer Questions

1. Why do Bear and Goat go into business?

_____

Text Evidence:

_____

_____

2. Who purchases Bear's baked potatoes?

_____

Text Evidence:

_____

_____

_____

3. What is the setting of this story?

_____

Text Evidence:

_____

4. Why don't Bear and Goat earn any money?

_____

_____

Text Evidence:

_____

_____

_____

Word	Examples
cardboard (KARD-bord)	This is cardboard. This is cardboard.
packaged (PA-kijd)	These are packaged in boxes. These are packaged in boxes.
recycle (ree-SY-kul)	You can recycle cardboard. You can recycle paper.
ship (SHIP)	You can ship a big box. You can ship a small box.

My Example	Definition
	cardboard, *noun* flat, stiff paper
	packaged, *verb* placed in a box
	recycle, *verb* to reuse
	ship, *verb* to send

From Pine Tree to Pizza Box

by Amy and Richard Hutchings

Trees can produce many things.

You can make paper and **cardboard** from trees.

First the trees are cut down and chopped into logs. Then the logs are turned into wood chips.

Next the wood chips become pulp. The pulp is pressed down to make cardboard.

Annotate

- Circle words that you have questions about.
- Underline the product that comes from trees.

5

The cardboard is then cut, shaped, and printed on.

6

These products are **packaged** in cardboard boxes.

7

You can use cardboard to **ship** and pack things.

8

You can **recycle** cardboard and paper products.

ThinkSpeakListen

Tell one thing about how cardboard is used.

133

From Pine Tree to Pizza Box

by Amy and Richard Hutchings

Trees are very important natural resources. People use the wood from some trees to make many things.

Pine trees are good trees for making paper and **cardboard** products.

First trees are cut down. Then they are chopped into logs. Logs are made into planks, boards, and wood chips.

Next the wood chips become a pulp. The pulp gets pressed into thin rolls of strong paper.

5

The cardboard can be cut, shaped, and printed on. It can then be folded into different types of finished products.

6

Cereal, sneakers, and games are **packaged** in cardboard boxes. So is pizza!

7

Cardboard is also used to **ship** things. When people move, they use a lot of cardboard boxes to pack their things.

8

It is important to **recycle** cardboard and other paper products. When cardboard is recycled, fewer trees need to be cut down.

ThinkSpeakListen

Explain why recycling is good for the environment.

From Pine Tree to Pizza Box

by Amy and Richard Hutchings

1   Trees are very important natural resources. People use the wood from some trees to make many things. Wood can be used to make furniture, pencils, paper, and more. Pine trees are good trees for making paper and **cardboard** products.

2   There are a lot of steps involved in turning a tree into a product, such as cardboard. First trees are cut down. Then they are chopped into logs. The logs are taken to a sawmill. The bark is removed. Logs are made into planks, boards, and wood chips.

food
air
shelter
fuel
wood products
paper and cardboard

3   Next the wood chips become a pulp. Wood pulp is soft and soggy. It gets pressed into thin rolls of strong paper. Three layers of paper at a time are then fed into a machine. The machine folds the paper. It glues the paper together. The pine tree is now cardboard!

4   The cardboard can be cut, shaped, and printed on. It can then be folded into different types of finished products.

5   Cardboard is a very lightweight, but strong, material. It is good for making boxes. Cereal, sneakers, and games are **packaged** in cardboard boxes. So is pizza!

6   Cardboard is also used to **ship** things. It is strong enough to protect whatever is packed inside. It is light enough so that it does not add much weight to a package.

7   It is important to **recycle** cardboard and other paper products. When something is recycled, its materials get used again. When cardboard is recycled, fewer trees need to be cut down.

Determine Meaning of Compound Words

Compound Word	Word Parts	Meaning

Identify Main Idea

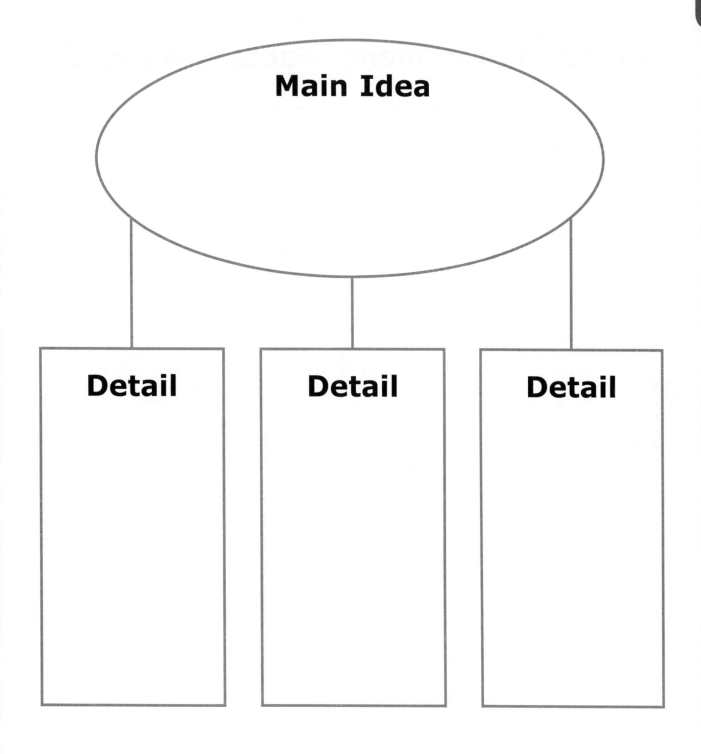

Main Idea

Detail

Detail

Detail

Analyze Author's Purpose

Author's Statement	Facts and Details

Draw an Inference

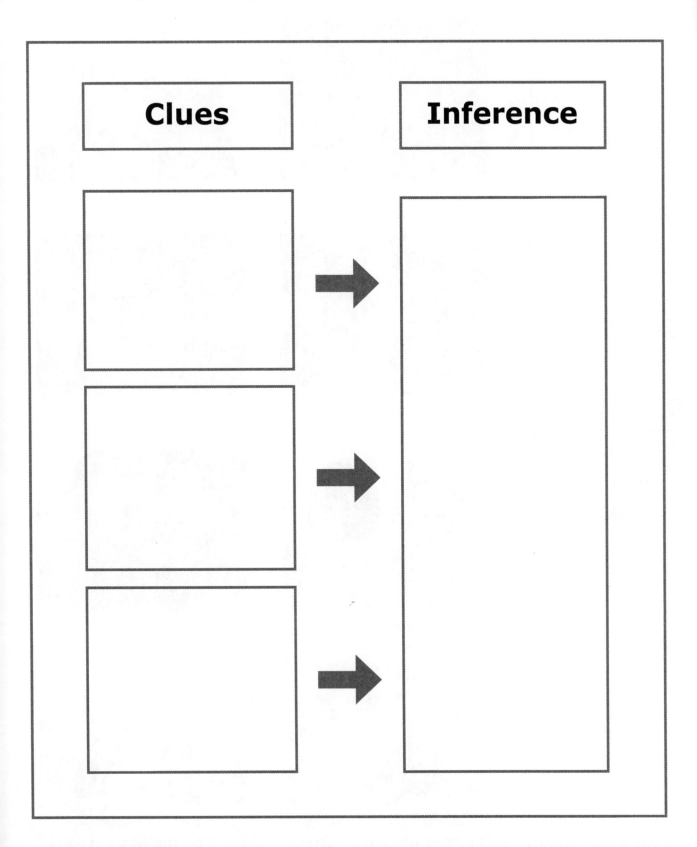

Word	Examples	
dinosaurs (DY-nuh-sorz)	These are dinosaurs.	These are dinosaurs.
fair (FAIR)	This is a fair.	This is a fair.
newspapers (NOOZ-pay-perz)	They have newspapers.	They use newspapers.
success (suk-SES)	The bake sale was a success.	The class trip was a success.

My Example	Definition
	dinosaurs, *noun* reptiles that lived millions of years ago
	fair, *noun* a special gathering
	newspapers, *noun* printed papers about the news
	success, *noun* an accomplishment

The Paper Dinosaurs

by Janine Scott

The students brought old **newspapers** to school.

A girl said, "Let's make paper **dinosaurs**."

The teacher said, "You can make your favorite dinosaur."

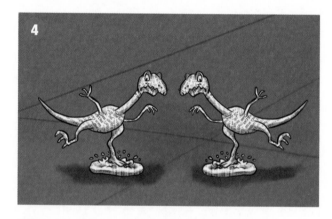

First the students tore the newspapers into strips. Next they rolled the pieces into balls.

Annotate

- Circle words that you have questions about.
- Underline what the students did after tearing the newspaper.

144

"We could make dinosaur footprints," said the girl.

"We could have a Dinosaur Dig at the **fair**," said a boy.

The students made footprints with the newspaper.

The Dinosaur Dig was a **success**!

ThinkSpeakListen

Who suggests making dinosaur footprints?

The Paper Dinosaurs

by Janine Scott

Mrs. Adams said,
"Let's make new things
from old **newspapers**.
Then we can sell what we
make at the school **fair**."

"Who has an idea?"
asked Mrs. Adams.

Amy said, "Let's make
paper **dinosaurs**."

Mrs. Adams told the class,
"Look at the dinosaur books
in the library. Choose your
favorite dinosaur to make."

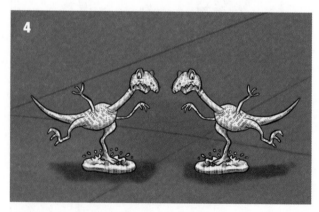

First they tore some
newspapers into strips. Next
they rolled other pieces into
balls. Before long, dinosaurs
took shape.

"Mrs. Adams," Amy cried. "I know another thing we could make with old newspapers. Dinosaur footprint fossils!"

"Great idea!" said Toby. "We could have a Dinosaur Dig at the fair. People could pay to dig for fossils buried in sand."

The class bubbled over with excitement. The children made footprint fossils in the mushy newspaper.

The Dinosaur Dig was a huge **success**. People loved "discovering" the footprint fossils.

ThinkSpeakListen

How did the students make the paper dinosaurs and footprint fossils? List the steps.

Notes

The Paper Dinosaurs

by Janine Scott

1   Mrs. Adams said, "Let's make new things from old **newspapers**. Then we can sell what we make at the school **fair**. That will help pay for a trip to the Science Museum. Who has an idea?"

2   Amy said, "Let's make paper **dinosaurs**."

3   Everyone loved that idea. With Mrs. Adams's help, Amy showed the class how to make a dinosaur from old newspapers. First they tore some newspapers into strips. Next they rolled other pieces into balls. "The balls will be the dinosaur's head and body," Amy explained. Then she dipped the paper strips into glue and placed them around the balls. Before long, a dinosaur took shape.

4   "It's your turn now," Mrs. Adams told the class. "Look at the dinosaur books in the library. Choose your favorite dinosaur to make."

5   "Mrs. Adams," Amy cried. "I know what we could make with old newspapers."

6   "What's that?" asked Mrs. Adams.

7   "Dinosaur footprint fossils!"
yelled Amy.

8   "Great idea!" said Toby. "We could
have a Dinosaur Dig at the fair. People
could pay to dig for fossils buried
in sand."

9   The class bubbled over with
excitement about the Dinosaur Dig. The
children researched dinosaur footprints on
the computer. Then the children made
footprint fossils in the mushy newspaper.

10   Toby was right. The Dinosaur Dig
was a huge **success**. People loved
"discovering" the footprint fossils.

Word Web

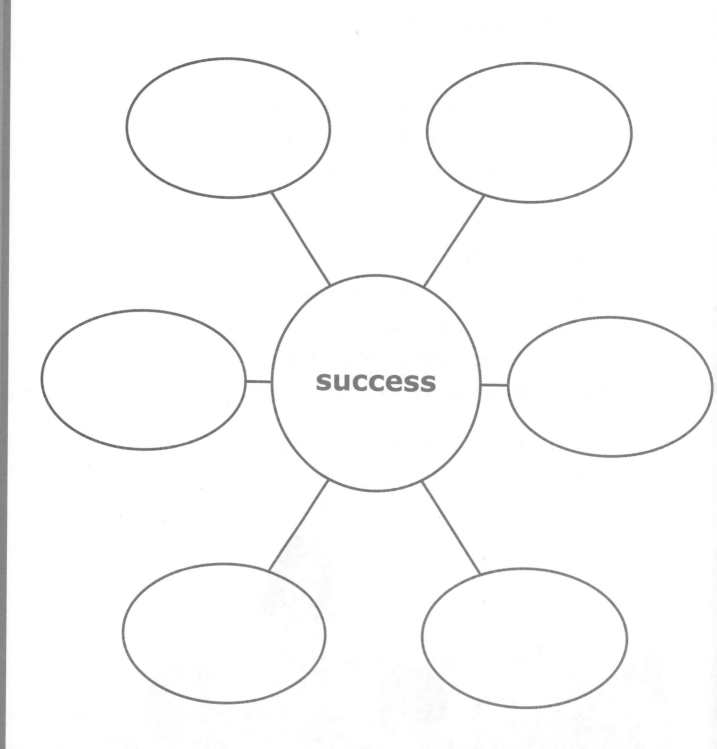

Recount Story Events

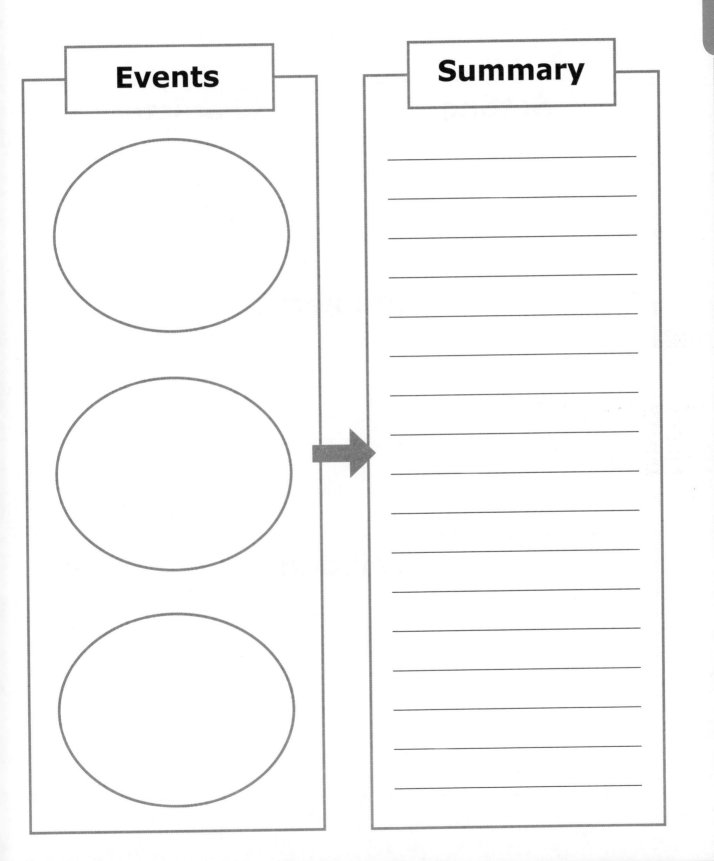

Events

Summary

Analyze Story Elements

Setting	Characters

Problem

Solution

Compare and Contrast

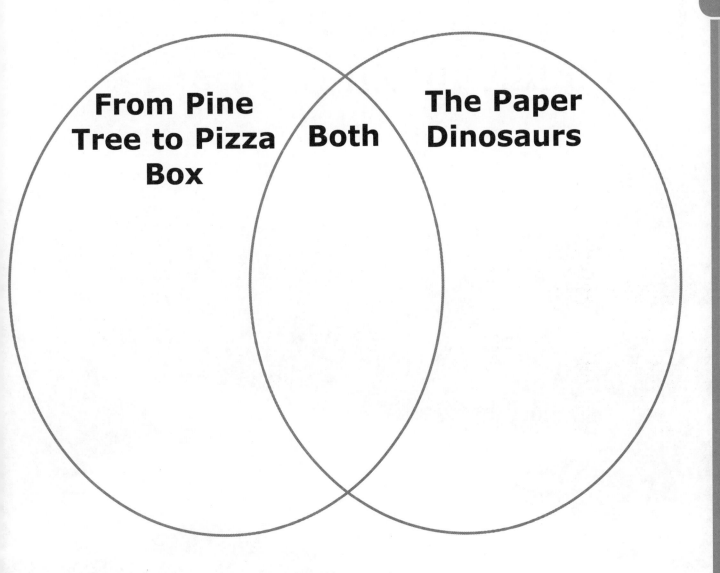

From Pine Tree to Pizza Box

Both

The Paper Dinosaurs

Essential Question

How can something old become new?

liquid

My Content Objectives

- Build vocabulary related to states of matter
- Understand how matter changes from one state to another

solid

gas

155

Word	Examples
corner (KOR-ner)	Here is a corner. Here is a corner.
folds (FOLDZ)	She folds the paper. He folds the paper.
origami (or-ih-GAH-mee)	He made origami. She made origami.
triangle (TRY-an-gul)	This is a triangle. This is a triangle.

My Example	Definition
	corner, *noun* a place where two sides meet
	folds, *verb* bends
	origami, *noun* the Japanese art of folding paper
	triangle, *noun* a shape with three sides and three corners

The Art of Origami

She makes **origami**.
Step 1:
She has a square.

Step 2:
She **folds** the square in half.
She has a **triangle**.

Step 3:
She folds the triangle in half.

Step 4:
She unfolds the triangle.

Annotate

- Circle words that you have questions about.
- Underline the direction after folding the triangle in half.

Step 5:

She folds two **corners**.

She has ears.

Step 6:

She folds the third corner.

Step 7:

She makes the eyes and nose.

She made a dog's face.

ThinkSpeakListen

What does the woman create with origami?

The Art of Origami

Today, you can try **origami** to create a dog's face. The directions are easy to follow.

Step 1: Begin with a square piece of paper.

Step 2: Fold the paper in half, top **corner** to bottom corner.

Step 3: Fold the **triangle** in half again, by folding the left point to the right point.

Step 4: Unfold the triangle. There will be a crease down the middle.

Step 5: To make the ears, fold both corners of the triangle down.

Step 6: Fold back the point at the bottom of the dog's head.

Step 7: Draw two eyes and a nose. Now your dog has a face.

You began with a square piece of paper and transformed it into a dog's face.

ThinkSpeakListen

What might happen if any of these steps were left out?

Remember to annotate as you read.

Notes

The Art of Origami

1   For thousands of years, people have been changing the size and shape of paper by folding it. **Origami**, the art of paper folding, began in China and then spread to Japan, where it became popular.

2   Today you can try your hand at this ancient craft by folding a square of paper to create a dog's face. The directions are easy to follow, so let's get started.

3   Step 1: Begin with a square piece of white or colored paper. A paper that is 8 square inches works well.

4   Step 2: **Fold** the paper in half from top **corner** to bottom corner. Now you have a **triangle**.

5   Step 3: Fold the triangle in half again, by folding the left point to the right point.

6   Step 4: Unfold the triangle. There will be a crease down the middle.

7   Step 5: To make the ears, fold both corners of the triangle down at an angle.

8   Step 6: Fold back the point at the bottom of the dog's head.

9   Step 7: Draw two eyes and a nose. Now your dog has a face.

10   You began with a square piece of paper and transformed it into a dog's face. How amazing is that!

Word Map

What does the word origami mean?

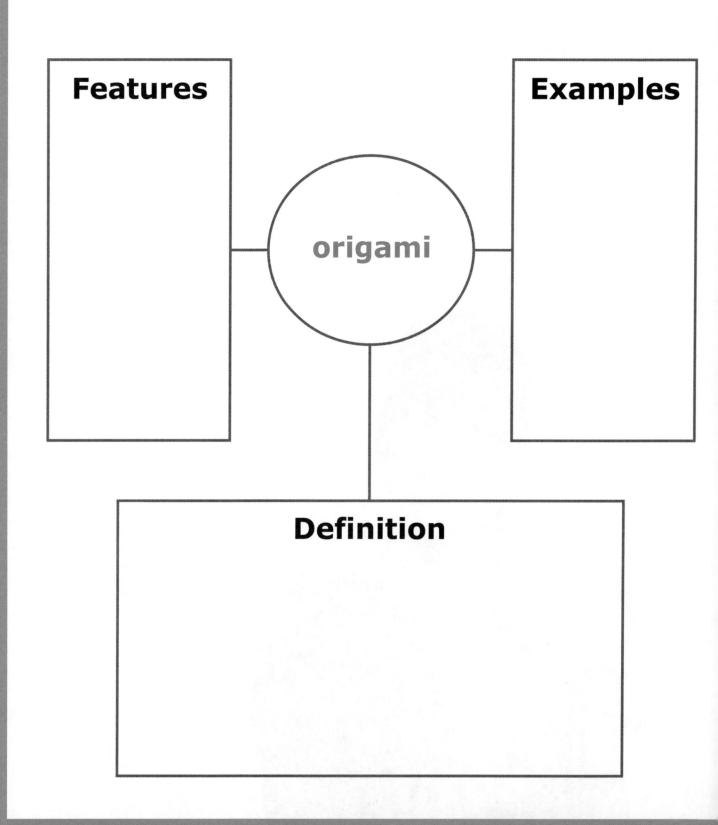

Features

Examples

origami

Definition

Identify Main Idea

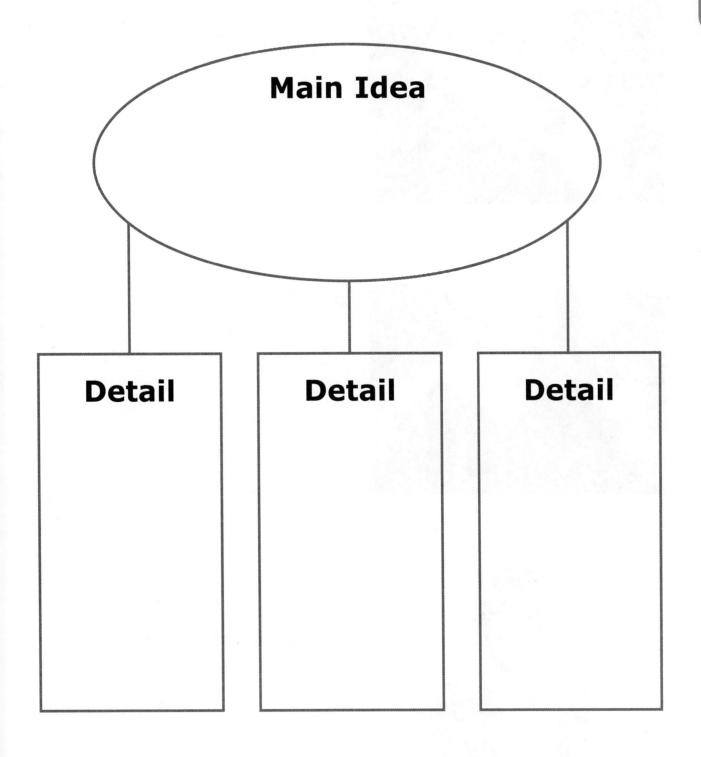

Main Idea

Detail

Detail

Detail

Use Graphic Features

1 **What does this photograph show?**

_____

_____

_____

2 **Describe what you see.**

_____

_____

_____

3 **What did the woman make with origami?**

_____

_____

_____

Analyze Steps in a Process

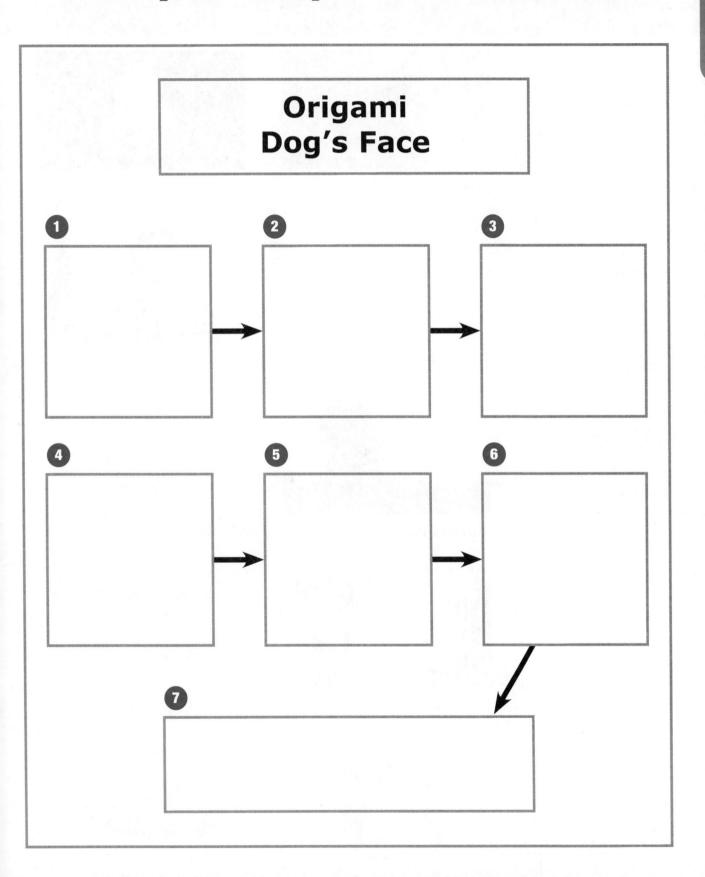

Origami Dog's Face

1

2

3

4

5

6

7

Word	Examples
gas (GAS)	The air is a gas. The steam is a gas.
liquid (LIH-kwid)	The water is a liquid. The juice is a liquid.
matter (MA-ter)	A tree is matter. A balloon is matter.
property (PRAH-per-tee)	Shape is a property. Size is a property.
solid (SAH-lid)	The ice is a solid. The rock is a solid.

My Example	Definition
	gas, *noun* a type of matter that does not have a fixed shape
	liquid, *noun* a type of matter that flows and takes the shape of its container
	matter, *noun* any substance that takes up space
	property, *noun* a quality or characteristic of matter
	solid, *noun* a type of matter that holds its shape

Changing Matter

by Jay Brewster

There are three states of **matter**. Each state has **properties**.

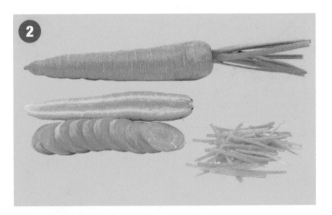

A **solid** has a shape. You can change the shape.

You can change the shape of a **liquid**.

You can change the shape of a **gas**, too.

Annotate

- (Circle) words that you have questions about.
- Underline what happens when matter changes temperature.

5

The temperature can change the state of matter.

6

A liquid can freeze.
It can become a solid.

7

A solid can melt.
It can become a liquid.

8

A liquid can boil.
It can become a gas.

ThinkSpeakListen

How does water change from one state of matter to another?

Changing Matter

by Jay Brewster

Everything in the world is made of **matter**. There are three states of matter: **solid**, **liquid**, and **gas**.

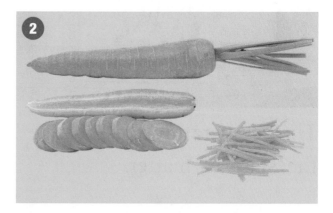

You can change the shape and size of matter. With an adult, you can cut a carrot into several small pieces or shred it.

Shape is another **property** of matter that can be changed. Pour water from a glass into the bowl. By pouring the water, you have changed its shape.

Gas can change its shape, too. Put a straw into a glass of milk and blow into the straw. The gas makes the bubbles in the milk.

5

When matter changes temperature, it can change from one state of matter into another. Water can exist in all three states of matter.

6

When water is very cold, it freezes. Frozen water, or ice, is solid matter that can have different shapes.

7

For ice to change from a solid back into a liquid, it needs to be heated up.

8

When water boils, it starts to bubble. Steam is liquid water that has turned into a gas.

ThinkSpeakListen

How might weather affect the states of water?

Notes

Changing Matter

by Jay Brewster

1   Everything in the world is made of **matter**. There are three kinds of matter: **solid**, **liquid**, and **gas**. All matter has properties, such as a size and a shape. Some properties can change. In addition, one kind of matter can sometimes change into another kind of matter.

2   Every solid, liquid, or gas has a certain size. You can change the size of matter. Here is one example. Suppose you have a carrot. A carrot is a solid piece of matter. You can change the size of the carrot by asking an adult to help you cut it into several small pieces or shred it.

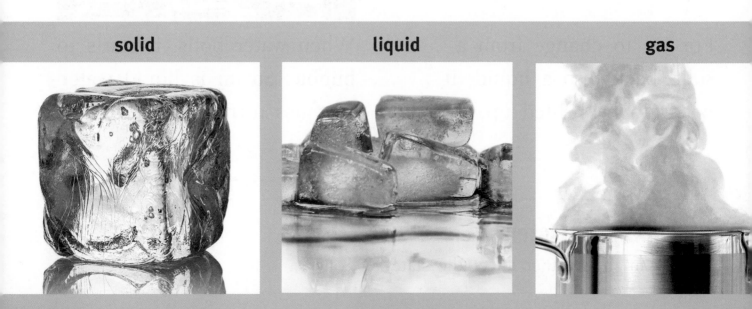

solid   liquid   gas

3   You can change the size of a liquid, too. Take a glass with water and pour half into another glass. You have changed the size of the liquid by dividing it.

4   Shape is another **property** of matter that can be changed. Get a bowl and pour the water into the bowl. By transferring the water from one container to another, you have changed its shape.

5   Gas can change its shape, too. Put a straw into a glass of milk and blow air into the straw. You will see bubbles moving around in the milk. By blowing into the milk, you made the gases in the glass move and change shape.

6   Water can exist in all three states of matter. When water is very cold, it freezes and becomes ice. Frozen water, or ice, is solid matter that can have different shapes. For ice to change from a solid back into a liquid, it needs to be heated up. When water in a pot on the stove starts to boil, it starts to bubble. Steam starts to rise from the pot. Steam is liquid water that has turned into a gas.

Word Web

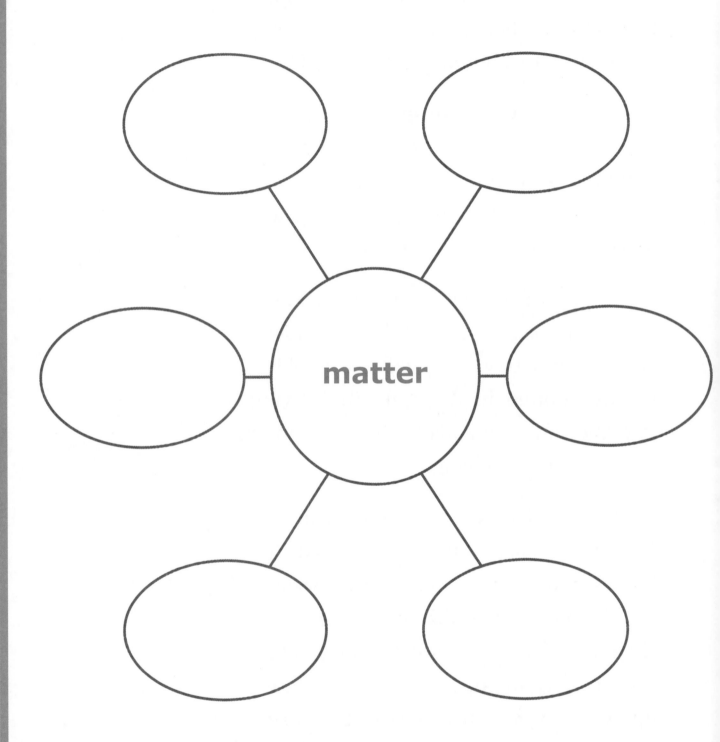

matter

Identify Main Idea

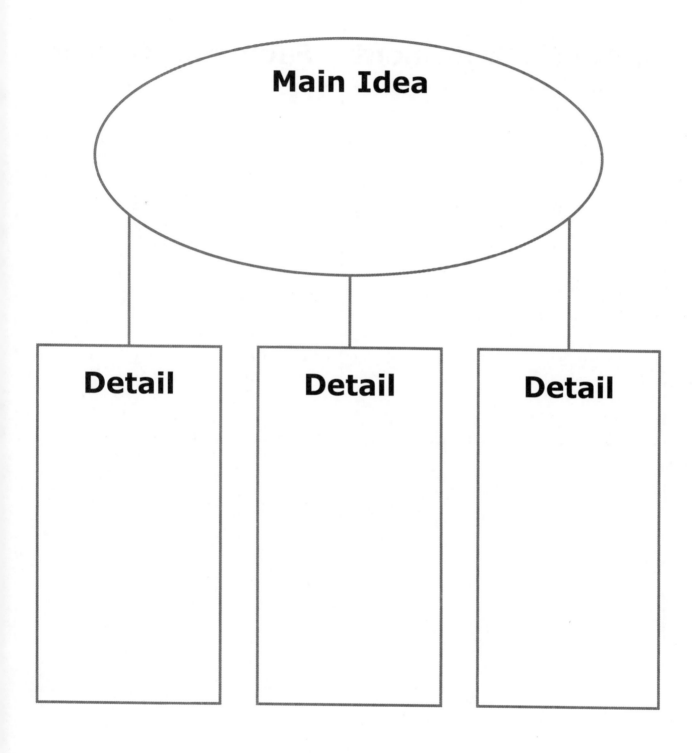

Main Idea

Detail

Detail

Detail

Identify Author's Purpose

Author's Statement	Facts and Details

Cause and Effect

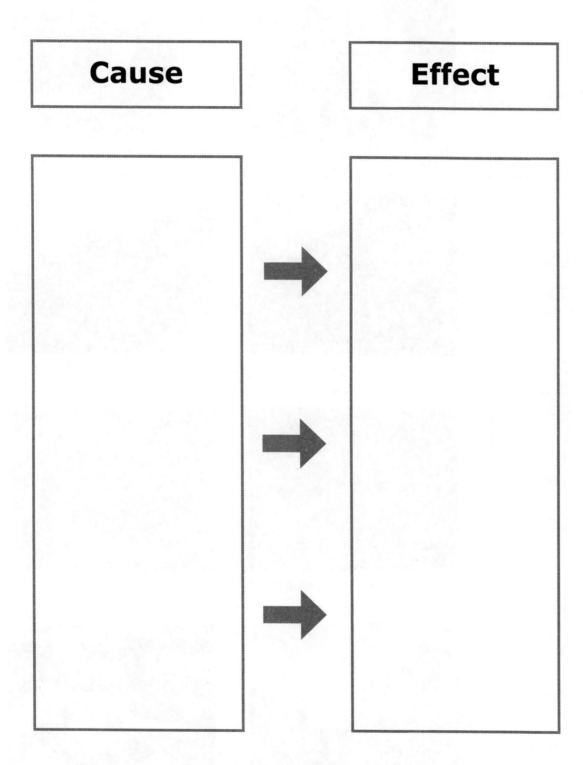

Word	Examples	
carve (KARV)	They carve the mountain.	They carve the rock.
mountain (MOWN-tun)	A mountain is big.	A mountain is rocky.
president (PREH-zih-dent)	Washington was a president.	Lincoln was a president.
sculpture (SKULP-cher)	 This is a sculpture.	 This is a sculpture.

My Example	Definition
	carve, *verb* to cut and shape a material
	mountain, *noun* a large, rocky hill
	president, *noun* an elected leader of a country
	sculpture, *noun* a carving of stone or wood

How Mount Rushmore Was Made by Kira Freed

This is a **sculpture**.

It is on a **mountain**.

He **carved** four **presidents**.

He made models.

Annotate
- Circle words that you have questions about.
- Underline who carved the rock.

The workers carved the rock.

They used tools to break the rock.

A lot of people worked on the sculpture.

The sculpture is Mount Rushmore.

ThinkSpeakListen

Summarize in a few sentences how Mount Rushmore was created.

How Mount Rushmore Was Made by Kira Freed

Gutzon Borglum was a sculptor, and Mount Rushmore is a piece of art that he created.

This **sculpture** is on a rock cliff in South Dakota. The **mountain** is tall enough to see from far away.

Borglum wanted the world to know about some great Americans. He decided to **carve** sculptures of four **presidents** on the mountain.

Borglum started by making drawings of the presidents. Then he used the drawings to make plaster models.

Workers used heavy drills to make holes in the rock. They put dynamite into the holes to blast away the outer rock.

Then Borglum himself worked on the rock. His artistry made the presidents look more alive.

A lot of people worked on Mount Rushmore. Many of the workers were ranchers, miners, or lumberjacks.

The Mount Rushmore sculpture took fourteen years to complete. Work began in 1927 and ended in 1941.

ThinkSpeakListen

What did Borglum and his workers do to the rock?

How Mount Rushmore Was Made

by Kira Freed

1   Mount Rushmore is a piece of art that Gutzon Borglum created. It is one of the largest sculptures in the world. The **sculpture** has the faces of four United States **presidents**. They are George Washington, Thomas Jefferson, Theodore Roosevelt, and Abraham Lincoln.

2   This sculpture is on a **mountain** in South Dakota. Borglum carved the presidents' faces very large so people could see them from far away.

3   Borglum wanted to create an important sculpture for this special place. He wanted the world to know about some great Americans.

4   Borglum started by making drawings of the presidents. Then he used the drawings to make plaster models. After Borglum finished the models, he was ready to start carving.

Mount Rushmore
National Memorial

5   Borglum didn't **carve** Mount Rushmore himself. He was in charge of the crew who did most of the work. Workers had to climb hundreds of stairs each day. They used heavy drills to make holes in the rock. They put dynamite into the holes to blast away the outer rock.

6   After the outer rock was gone, Borglum himself worked on the rock. His artistry made the presidents look more alive.

7   Nearly 400 men and women worked on Mount Rushmore. The workers were not artists—many were ranchers, miners, or lumberjacks. When the project began, Borglum taught them how to carve rock.

8   The Mount Rushmore sculpture took fourteen years to complete. Work began in 1927 and ended in 1941.

Determine Word Meanings

What does the word sculpture mean?

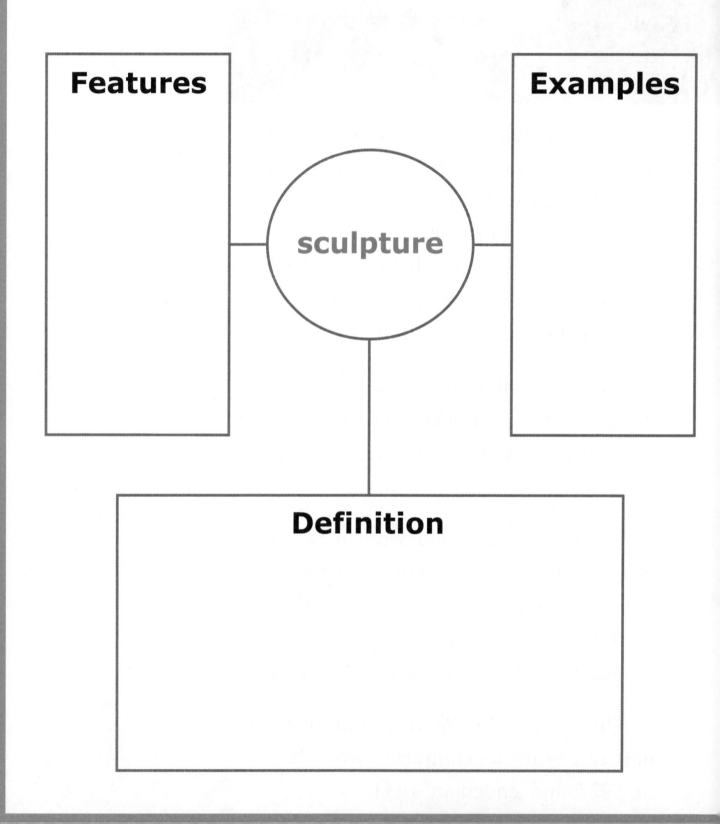

Features

Examples

sculpture

Definition

Identify Main Idea

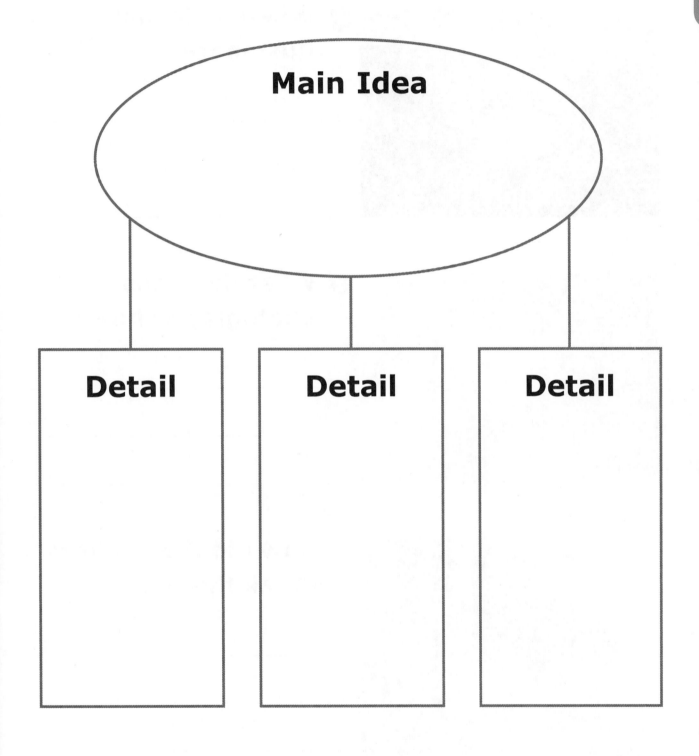

Main Idea

Detail

Detail

Detail

Use Graphic Features

1 Where is Mount Rushmore?

_____

_____

_____

2 What does this photograph show?

_____

_____

_____

3 How did the workers break the rock?

_____

_____

_____

Compare and Contrast

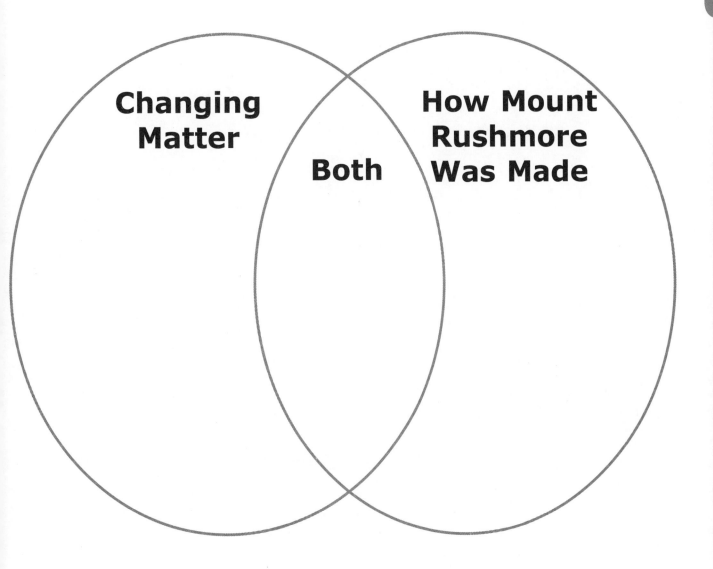

Changing Matter

Both

How Mount Rushmore Was Made